Famous Unanswered Prayers

by Warren W. Wiersbe
General Director
Back to the Bible

Back to the Bible

Lincoln, Nebraska 68501

45,000 printed to date—1986
(5-4921—45M—76)
ISBN 0-8474-6514-4

Printed in the United States of America

Contents

Chapter 1

Barriers to Answered Prayer

Just as fathers and mothers desire to meet the needs of their children as an expression of their love for them, so also our Heavenly Father delights in answering our prayers. However, prayer is much more than our coming to God and making requests of Him. Prayer is a precious experience of communion and worship—getting to know our Father, and ourselves, better. Prayer is one of the highest privileges we have in the Christian life, and God delights in answering prayer. Our Lord Jesus said, "If ye then, being evil, know how to give good gifts unto your children, how much more shall your Father which is in heaven give good things to them that ask him?" (Matt. 7:11).

This brings us to the great problem of unanswered prayer. Some people will argue that God *always* answers prayer. He either says yes, no or wait. However, I believe this is a rather shallow way of dealing with the problem of unanswered prayer. It is true that God sometimes delays in answering our prayers. His timing is different from our own. When Lazarus was very ill, his sisters, Mary and Martha, sent for the Lord Jesus. However, the Lord deliberately waited to come. When He finally arrived at Bethany, Lazarus had been in the grave for four days. Christ purposely delayed in order to bring greater glory to God by raising this man from the dead (see John 11:1-44). In this case the Lord delayed because the timing was not right for God's purposes to be fulfilled.

In addition to timing, God sometimes delays or denies a particular request because He has a greater blessing waiting for us. Many times we are like children, who want to have some cheap little toy right now. Like a good parent, our Heavenly Father does not give us what we want at that time because He has something even better planned for us.

Thus, even when we are praying in the Lord's will, we may have some requests changed or delayed for our good. But these are still forms of answered prayer. However, the Bible teaches us that there are times when God does not hear or answer our prayers. These unanswered prayers are not caused by His inability to hear or respond but are the result of barriers that we have erected in our hearts. Therefore, the problem of unanswered prayer is really our problem—not God's. The Lord will not answer prayer just to pamper us. While He knows and sees everything and is all-powerful, God will not answer our prayers if they are out of His will or inconsistent with His nature.

What are the barriers that cause our line of communication with God to be severed? While the Bible describes a number of hindrances to prayer, four in particular pose serious problems to our prayer life.

Let's examine some of these barriers to answered prayer.

Known Sin

The first barrier to answered prayer is *known sin in our lives.* Psalm 66:18 states, "If I regard iniquity in my heart, the Lord will not hear me." In this passage, the psalmist is not talking about possessing a sinful nature. Every person who has ever walked on this earth has a sinful nature, with one important exception—Jesus Christ. He "knew no sin" (II Cor. 5:21). He "did no sin" (I Pet. 2:22). In Him there was no sin (I John 3:5).

But while we possess sinful natures, this alone does not hinder our prayers. It is *regarding* our sins that causes our prayers to go unanswered. The word "regard" means to know that something is present, to approve it but do nothing about it. If I'm aware of some sin in my heart and acknowledge its presence yet am unwilling to face it honestly and do something about it, then God will not hear me when I pray.

The reason for God's response is obvious. We are being hypocrites. First John 1:6 says, "If we say that we have fellowship with him, and walk in darkness, we lie, and do not the truth." We are saying one thing but practicing another. Ignoring our sins is a serious offense in God's eyes, for "if we say that we have not sinned, we make him a liar, and his word is not in us" (v. 10).

Job also confirmed the danger of being hypocritical. He stated, "For what is the hope of the hypocrite, though he hath gained, when God taketh away his soul? Will God hear his cry when trouble cometh upon him?" (Job 27:8,9). Many people today are so busy accumulating material wealth that they ignore their sins—and God. When they are in trouble and about to die, then they cry out to God for help. But the Lord says to them, in effect, "Look, you didn't cry out to Me or do anything about your sins before. Why should I hear you now?"

When we are regarding, or cherishing, a known sin in our hearts, the Lord will not hear or answer us. To cherish a sin means to practice it secretly, to think about it, to enjoy the memory of it, to be unwilling to face it honestly. We must not allow sins to remain in our lives in this manner but must deal with them drastically. Jesus said, "If your right eye is causing you to stumble, pluck it out. If your right hand causes you to sin, cut it off" (see Matt. 5:29,30). Obviously, our Lord was not speaking in literal terms. Physical surgery does not produce spirituality. Instead, He's saying to us, "Deal drastically with sin before it spreads and destroys your entire being."

This is why, when we come to God in prayer, we need to have a time of confession and cleansing first. "If we confess our sins, he is faithful and just to forgive us our sins, and to cleanse us from all unrighteousness" (I John 1:9). In the Old Testament tabernacle and temple, before the priests could enter the Holy Place and burn incense at the golden altar (representing the prayers of the people), they had to stop at the laver and wash their hands and feet. Even though they were serving the Lord, the priests were still defiled. Therefore, before they could enter the holy presence of God, they had to come for cleansing at the laver. So also you and I need to have cleansing. "Wash me, and I shall be whiter than snow" (Ps. 51:7).

Selfishness

The first barrier to answered prayer is known sin that we cherish and defend in our lives. A second barrier that hinders our prayers is *selfishness*. James pointed out that when we are selfish in our praying, God will not hear us: "From whence come wars and fightings among you? come they not hence, even of your lusts that war in your members?" (James 4:1). The word "lust" in this verse means "pleasures." The passage goes on to say, "Ye lust, and have not: ye kill, and desire to have, and cannot obtain: ye fight and war, yet ye have not, because ye ask not. Ye ask, and receive not, because ye ask amiss, that ye may consume it upon your lusts" (vv. 2,3). This is a rather outspoken statement, isn't it? Apparently, the congregation that James was writing to was having some painful discussions, divisions and disputes. One of the reasons they were divided and were disputing with each other was because they were not praying as they should. They were praying selfishly.

While it is not wrong for God's people to pray for themselves, it is wrong to put our requests so far ahead of God's requests that we become selfish. In

9

the Lord's Prayer, we notice that God's concerns come before ours: "Our Father which art in heaven, Hallowed be thy name. Thy kingdom come. Thy will be done" (Matt. 6:9,10). Once we have prayed for God's concerns, we can then say, "Give us this day our daily bread" (v. 11). This shows us that it isn't wrong to pray for ourselves. Many people in the Bible did so. When you read the Book of the Psalms, you find David often praying for himself for spiritual cleansing, for power, for physical protection and for deliverance from his enemies. In the New Testament, our Lord Jesus prayed for Himself on several occasions. Likewise, Paul prayed for himself as well as for others.

As we have noted earlier, God enjoys answering prayer and meeting our needs. Selfish praying, however, is not the same as praying for ourselves. We pray for ourselves that we might be able to serve others. We pray for our needs that we might be able to meet the needs of others. This is vastly different from the attitude portrayed in James 4:2,3: "Ye have not, because ye ask not. Ye ask, and receive not, because ye ask amiss, that ye may consume it upon your lusts." In this case, our sole purpose for praying is to satisfy our own pleasures and desires.

What are the evidences of selfish praying? First, we become hard to live with. We are constantly fighting and disputing with others. We also want *our* pleasures to be fulfilled. We are not interested in glorifying God—only in pacifying ourselves.

But the purpose of prayer is not self-gratification.

The purpose of prayer is to accomplish the will of God. The Apostle John made this very clear when he wrote: "And this is the confidence that we have in him, that, if we ask any thing according to his will, he heareth us: and if we know that he hear us, whatsoever we ask, we know that we have the petitions that we desired of him" (I John 5:14,15). Thus, we see that when we are asking according to *the Lord's will*, God promises to grant our petitions.

It has been well said that the purpose of prayer is not to get man's will done in heaven. It's to get God's will done on earth. This is why we must search the Scriptures and find out what God's will really is.

Selfishness is a barrier to answered prayer. Sometimes our prayers can be selfish, and we don't even realize it. This is why we must seek the Spirit's discernment when we pray. In addition, we must have a life that is filled with the Word of God in order to know how to pray in the will of God.

Disagreement in the Home

A third barrier to answered prayer is *disagreement in the home*. The basis for this truth is found in I Peter 3:7, where the Apostle Peter said, "Likewise, ye husbands, dwell with them [your wives] according to knowledge, giving honour unto the wife, as unto the weaker vessel, and as being heirs together of the grace of life; that your prayers be not hindered." The word "hindered" has an interesting meaning in the original. It means to break up a road so that the army can't get through. In ancient war-

11

fare, this method was often used. The soldiers would block the road with rocks, trees and other barriers to prevent the opposing army from advancing. Thus, I Peter 3:7 is telling husbands and wives that if they are not getting along with each other, their prayers will be hindered. They will be putting up barricades and barriers along the road that will prevent God from answering their prayers.

Prayer is so important in the home. Husbands and wives need to pray together daily. However, I am amazed at how many Christian husbands and wives have ignored this aspect of their marriage. My wife and I have often told young couples that they must build their marriage on the foundation of their love for the Lord Jesus and their faithfulness to Him. Any other foundation simply won't last.

This passage in I Peter shows us the importance of our relationship with *all* people, and especially with our husband or wife. We must be very careful how we treat other people. If we are not dwelling together according to the guidelines in the Word of God and are not honoring our spouses and others as equal heirs in Christ, then God will not answer our prayers.

Not only does this hurt the Christian home, but it affects the church as well. If a pastor, teacher or church leader is not praying and getting along with his family at home, then his private and public prayers will not go very far. Before we can have revival in our churches, we must first have revival in our marriages and homes. We must begin reading the Word of God and praying together at home before our ministry in the church can be everything it should be.

Rejection of God's Word

Harboring known sins in our hearts, praying self-ishly and having disagreement in the home all cause our prayers to go unanswered. A fourth hindrance to our prayer life is *rejection of God's Word.* We read in Proverbs 28:9: "He that turneth away his ear from hearing the law, even his prayer shall be abomination." Ignoring and rejecting the Word of God is a barrier to answered prayer.

The Word of God and prayer always go together. Jesus said, "If ye abide in me, and my words abide in you, ye shall ask what ye will, and it shall be done unto you" (John 15:7). In Acts 6:4 we find the early church leaders devoting themselves continually to the ministry of prayer and the Word of God. The Word of God and prayer must go together because the Bible reveals to us God's mind, heart and will. Once we know this, we can then claim His promises, His will and His provision for our needs in prayer.

Prayer is not something we do ourselves. Prayer is the result of the Spirit of God using the Word of God in our lives. If we reject the Word, God cannot hear and answer prayer. He would be violating the holiness of His nature in doing so.

God desires to answer our prayers. Unfortunately, He is not always able to do so because we have placed a barrier between ourselves and Him. Refusing to confess and forsake known sins in our lives, praying with selfish motives, harboring disagreement in the home and ignoring the Word of God are all barriers to our prayer lives. Perhaps we need to examine our hearts and lives and ask God to tear down some of these barriers. "Break down ev'ry idol, cast out ev'ry foe—/ Now wash me and I shall be whiter than snow."

Chapter 2

God Told Moses No!

(Deuteronomy 3:23-28)

We usually think of Moses as the great leader and lawgiver. Of course, he was a magnificent leader and great lawgiver. But he was also a teacher, a prophet and a mighty prayer warrior. We find many examples of Moses' dedicated prayer life in the Old Testament. When God sent the plagues on Egypt, it was Moses' prayers to the Lord that frequently caused the plagues to cease (see Ex. 7:14—12:36). When the Amalekites attacked the Israelites in the wilderness, Moses went up on the mountaintop and lifted up his hands in prayer. As long as Moses' hands were raised, the Israelites were victorious down in the valley (see 17:8-16).

When the nation of Israel sinned greatly against the Lord by worshiping the golden calf, it was Moses, the intercessor, who spared them (see 32:7-14). He went back to Mount Sinai and prayed to God on behalf of the people (see vv. 30-35). When God smote Miriam with leprosy for criticizing Moses, he was the one who prayed for her, and God healed her (see Num. 12:1-16). At Kadesh-barnea, when the Jewish people had disobeyed God by

15

refusing to enter the Promised Land, Moses once again interceded on their behalf, and the Lord spared the people (see 14:1-21). When the Israelites were bitten by fiery serpents, it was Moses' intercession that brought healing (see 21:5-9).

It is interesting that Moses was the great intercessor. People criticized him. They complained about what he did. They took him for granted, and yet if it had not been for the prayers of Moses, where would the nation of Israel have been? I think this is often true of families and churches as well. Children often don't appreciate the prayers of their parents and grandparents. Some people may even be reaping the benefits of their great-grandparents' prayers. God makes it clear that prayer is vital in the home and in the church. Therefore, we shouldn't take the prayers of our families or our pastors for granted, for if we have praying parents and spiritual leaders, we have the answer to every problem and the provision for every need.

Moses often prayed for others, and God gave him what he requested. But not all of Moses' prayers were answered. We discover that when Moses made one particular request for himself, God refused to grant his petition. In Deuteronomy 3:23-28 we read: "And I besought the Lord at that time, saying, O Lord God, thou hast begun to shew thy servant thy greatness, and thy mighty hand: for what God is there in heaven or in earth, that can do according to thy works, and according to thy might? I pray thee, let me go over, and see the good land that is beyond Jordan, that goodly mountain, and Lebanon. But the Lord was wroth [angry] with me for your sakes, and would not hear me: and the Lord said unto me, Let it suffice thee; speak no more unto me of this matter. Get thee up into the top of Pisgah, and lift up thine eyes westward, and northward, and southward, and eastward, and behold it with thine eyes: for thou shalt not go over this Jordan. But charge Joshua, and encourage him, and strengthen him: for he shall cause them to inherit the land which thou shalt see."

Why was this simple request denied by God? To understand the reason for this unanswered prayer, we need to look back at another incident in Moses' life that brought about God's response. As we do, we will discover some important reasons why some of our prayers are not answered by God.

The Meaning of Prayer

This painful experience of Moses reveals to us some important reminders that will help us in our prayer life and in our walk with the Lord. Moses' unanswered prayer reminds us, first of all, of *the meaning of prayer*.

What is prayer? Prayer is asking God to accomplish His will. Prayer is not arguing with the Lord. When Moses asked God to allow him to cross the Jordon River into Canaan, he already knew what God's will was in the matter. As a result of a previous sin, the Lord had forbidden Moses to enter the Promised Land. We read in Numbers 20: "And the Lord spake unto Moses, saying, Take the rod, and gather thou the assembly together, thou, and

17

Aaron thy brother, and speak ye unto the rock before their eyes; and it shall give forth his water, and thou shalt bring forth to them water out of the rock: so thou shalt give the congregation and their beasts drink. And Moses took the rod from before the Lord, as he commanded him. And Moses and Aaron gathered the congregation together before the rock, and he said unto them, Hear now, ye rebels; must we fetch you water out of this rock? And Moses lifted up his hand, and with his rod he smote the rock twice: and the water came out abundantly, and the congregation drank, and their beasts also. And the Lord spake unto Moses and Aaron, Because ye believed me not, to sanctify me in the eyes of the children of Israel, therefore ye shall not bring this congregation into the land which I have given them" (vv. 7-12).

Moses and Aaron sinned against God in two ways. First, Moses had disobeyed God's direct command to speak to the rock and had struck it with the rod instead. Second, they had taken credit for producing the water rather than giving the praise to the Lord. Because of their sin, God had made it clear to Moses and Aaron that they would not lead the people into the land of Canaan. Moses knew the will of God, and yet in Deuteronomy 3 we find him trying to change God's mind.

Of course, some may argue that God had changed His mind before when Moses prayed to Him on behalf of the people. For example, when the Lord was preparing to destroy the people at Kadesh-barnea, Moses pleaded with Him, saying,

"Now if thou shalt kill all this people as one man, then the nations which have heard the fame of thee will speak, saying, Because the Lord was not able to bring this people into the land which he sware unto them, therefore he hath slain them in the wilderness. . . . Pardon, I beseech thee, the iniquity of this people according unto the greatness of thy mercy" (Num. 14:15,16,19). While God did pardon the people for the present, He was not really changing His mind. He did ultimately destroy the Israelites because of their sin, allowing only the new generation to go into the land (see vv. 20-35).

Moses knew that God had already forbidden him to enter Canaan, yet he thought he could change the Lord's mind. While it would have been possible for God to change His mind and answer Moses' prayer, to do so would have contradicted His nature of justice. By allowing Moses to enter the land even after he had sinned, God would have been discriminating against the Children of Israel. Because of their sin in refusing to believe and honor God at Kadesh-barnea, an entire generation had been condemned to die in the wilderness. God would also have been discriminating against Aaron. Because of his sin at the rock of Meribah, Aaron had not been allowed to enter the land. God had spoken to Moses and Aaron on Mount Hor near Edom, saying, "Aaron shall be gathered unto his people: for he shall not enter into the land which I have given unto the children of Israel, because ye rebelled against my word at the water of Meribah" (Num. 20:24). After passing his duties as high priest on to his son Eleazar, Aaron had died on the mountain (see vv. 27-29). Since Aaron and the whole generation of Israelites had died, would it have been fair for God to have spared Moses? For that matter, because of his position of authority and leadership, the consequences of his sin would have been even greater. Thus, God could not overlook Moses' sin and still be fair and just.

Even though Moses was a great intercessor, he had forgotten the meaning of prayer. Like Moses, we all need to be reminded of the purpose of prayer. It has often been said, "Prayer is not overcoming God's reluctance but is taking hold of God's willingness." Prayer is not arguing with the Lord or twisting His arm in order to get what we want. Prayer is asking God to perform His will in our lives and then accepting His will. When we are praying within the will of God, we will receive an answer: "And this is the confidence that we have in him, that, if we ask any thing according to his will, he heareth us: and if we know that he hear us, whatsoever we ask, we know that we have the petitions that we desired of him" (I John 5:14,15).

The Seriousness of Sin

Moses' experience with unanswered prayer reminds us not only of the meaning of prayer but also of *the seriousness of sin.* When the Israelites complained to Moses about their lack of water, God commanded Moses to speak to a rock, promising that water would come forth from it (see Num. 20:8). This was not the first time God had provided

20

water from a rock (see Ex. 17:5-7). On the first occasion, the Lord had commanded Moses to strike the rock. Now, instead of obeying the Lord's command to speak, Moses relied on his past experience and struck the rock twice. While God still kept His promise and gave them water from the rock, He made it clear to Moses that he had committed a serious sin.

Why was this sin so serious? Why was it so important for Moses to speak to the rock rather than to strike it? Moses' disobedience revealed his lack of faith in the power of God. Rather than trusting God to do what He said He would, Moses tried to rely on methods that had worked in the past. In the Lord's eyes, Moses and Aaron had committed the sin of unbelief. God told them, "Because ye believed me not, to sanctify me in the eyes of the children of Israel, therefore ye shall not bring this congregation into the land which I have given them" (Num. 20:12).

Moses' sin of unbelief was serious in another respect. The Lord had provided water from the rock on both occasions in order to give the people a picture of Jesus Christ, the Rock from which the living water of the Holy Spirit flows. It was an illustration of how Christ would be smitten once on the cross—not over and over again—in order that the people might have the Living Water. From that point on, it would not be necessary to strike the Rock again. Instead, the people could speak to the Rock and receive the fullness and power of the Holy Spirit. Striking the rock speaks of Christ's death on

21

the cross; speaking to the rock speaks of His heavenly ministry. We come to Him, and He gives us what we need. When Moses disobeyed God's command and struck the rock rather than speaking to it, he ruined the beautiful picture God was seeking to portray.

Not only had Moses committed the sin of unbelief in refusing to obey God's specific instructions, but he was also guilty of the sin of pride. The Lord told Moses, "You did not sanctify me in the eyes of the Children of Israel" (see v. 12). Prior to that time, Moses had been a very meek and humble man (see 12:3), but his meekness disappeared at that instant. He temporarily forgot that the purpose of leadership is to glorify God. He lost his temper and called the people rebels, saying, "Must we fetch you water out of this rock?" (20:10). Moses took credit for the miracle God was about to perform, glorifying himself rather than the Lord.

It's interesting to note how many people in the Bible failed in their strengths—not in their weaknesses. Moses' great strength was his meekness, and Satan used pride to cause him to stumble. Abraham's strength lay in his great faith. That's where he failed. Twice he lied about his wife, Sarah (see Gen. 12:10—13:4; 20:1-18). David's great strength was his integrity. He was a man after God's own heart. But he forgot his integrity and began to scheme in order to get Uriah's wife (see II Sam. 11). Peter's great strength was his courage. But in his moment of testing, he denied knowing Christ three times out of fear for his life (see Luke 22:54-62).

The reason Moses' sin was so serious in God's eyes was because it was a sin of rebellion, as well as one of unbelief and pride. Numbers 27:12-14 tells us, "And the Lord said unto Moses, Get thee up into this mount Abarim, and see the land which I have given unto the children of Israel. And when thou hast seen it, thou also shalt be gathered unto thy people, as Aaron thy brother was gathered. For ye rebelled against my commandment in the desert of Zin."

Of course, the people were partly to blame for Moses' sin. Like all leaders, Moses had been provoked at times by the Children of Israel. In Deuteronomy 1:37 Moses stated, "Also the Lord was angry with me for your sakes, saying, Thou also shalt not go in thither." We find a further explanation in Psalm 106:32,33: "They angered him also at the waters of strife, so that it went ill with Moses for their sakes: because they provoked his spirit, so that he spake unadvisedly with his lips."

Sometimes the people of God create problems for the servant of God. That's why it is so important for us to be patient with our pastors and church leaders. We need to love and support them rather than complain about them and to them. May we never be guilty of contributing to a person's fall into sin.

The Grace of God

This incident in the life of Moses teaches us not only the meaning of prayer and the seriousness of sin but also *the grace of God* in answering, or not

23

answering, our prayers. Where sin abounds, grace abounds even more (see Rom. 5:20). While God, in His grace, forgave Moses for his sin, God, in His government, forced Moses to reap what he had sown.

But the Lord had another reason for refusing to answer Moses' prayer to enter the Promised Land. He did not answer his prayer for *our* sake. Once again God used this incident in the life of Moses as an object lesson for future generations. Moses was not allowed to lead the people into the Promised Land because he represented the Law. God wanted to teach us that we cannot claim our inheritance by obeying the Law. Instead, God appointed Joshua to lead the people, enabling them to obtain their inheritance. Joshua is a picture of our Lord Jesus Christ. The name Joshua means "Jehovah is salvation." Joshua is the Old Testament version of Jesus, the Living Word of the New Testament. The Lord used Joshua instead of Moses to show us that we do not claim our spiritual inheritance through the Law but through the victory of Jesus Christ.

How close are you to the Promised Land (your inheritance in Christ)? Canaan is not a picture of heaven; it is a picture of our inheritance in Christ. Some people know nothing about the land. They are lost. Others know about it, but they want to go back as the mixed multitude Moses lead out of Egypt wanted to do. These Christians have seen and tasted a part of the victorious life in Christ, but they want to go back into the world. They are like the ten spies who died. They went into the land, tasted its fruit and saw its blessing but didn't claim it because of their unbelief. Still other people live on the border of the land like the two and a half tribes that lived on the other side of the Jordan River. They are close to the land (life in Christ) but still don't possess it.

Like Moses, many of us are not able to enter the land and experience the blessings of answered prayer because we have forgotten the meaning of prayer or have some sin hindering our prayers. Instead of arguing with God or trying to convince Him to give us our desires, we need to yield to His design, saying, "Thy will be done." In addition, we need to examine our hearts to see if we are guilty of the sins of unbelief, pride, rebellion or any others that could be standing between us and God. Before we can approach the throne of grace and commune with the Lord, we must have our hearts cleansed of every sin.

When we are struggling in the throes of unanswered prayer, we need to remember that God's grace is still sufficient. Even though Moses was unable to enter the land during his lifetime, he was privileged to be with Christ at the Mount of Transfiguration, entering the land at last (see Matt. 17:1-3). Likewise, while we may have to reap the results of what we have sown, we can be strengthened in the knowledge that we have been forgiven by God when we acknowledge our sin before Him. "Let us therefore come boldly unto the throne of grace, that we may obtain mercy, and find grace to help in time of need" (Heb. 4:16).

Chapter 3

Presumptuous Praying

(Deuteronomy 1:41-46)

Our God is gracious and patient. Often He gives us, His people, another opportunity if we fail. When Abraham lied to the king of Egypt, saying that Sarah was his sister, he was able to return to the altar and confess it to God (see Gen. 12:10—13:4). Isaac also lied about his wife, but God forgave him and gave him a fresh beginning (see 26:6-12). Jacob schemed to take away the inheritance and blessing from his brother, Esau, yet God still honored the Abrahamic covenant through Jacob (see 27:1—28:4). Even Jonah, who sinned so grievously against the Lord by refusing to take His message to Nineveh, was given another chance. "And the word of the Lord came unto Jonah the second time, saying, Arise, go" (Jon. 3:1,2). Of course, the classic example in the Bible is the Apostle Peter, who denied the Lord three times (see Luke 22:54-62). And yet God did not forsake him. The Lord Jesus forgave Peter, restored him and gave him another chance.

We do indeed serve a loving, merciful and forgiving God. However, we must never presume upon the grace of God. Nor should we assume that, because we've confessed our sins, we will not experience any discipline for our actions. God willingly forgives us, but He does not guarantee that our lives will remain the way they were before we sinned.

The nation of Israel learned this lesson the hard way at Kadesh-barnea. They had come to the border of the Promised Land and had sent spies in to survey the situation (see Num. 13:1-25). The spies returned with the report that it was indeed a good land. However, ten of the spies warned that the Canaanites were too strong for them to conquer (see vv. 26-33). Joshua and Caleb tried to convince them to trust God for the victory, saying, "Let us go up at once, and possess it; for we are well able to overcome it" (v. 30). The Children of Israel refused to believe God and instead listened to the advice of the ten spies. They wanted to return to Egypt (see 14:1-4).

Because of their unbelief, God had to discipline the Israelites. The ten unbelieving spies died immediately (see vv. 36,37), and God condemned the rest of the people to wander in the wilderness until every person above the age of 20 had died (see vv. 28-35). The Children of Israel had to wait 40 years before the new generation could enter the Promised Land.

After the nation heard the word of the Lord through Moses, His servant, the people then decided to try to conquer the land on their own. We read in Numbers 14:39-45: "And Moses told these sayings unto all the children of Israel: and the people mourned greatly. And they rose up early in the morning, and gat them up into the top of the moun-

27

tain, saying, Lo, we be here, and will go up unto the place which the Lord hath promised: for we have sinned. And Moses said, Wherefore now do ye transgress the commandment of the Lord? but it shall not prosper. Go not up, for the Lord is not among you; that ye be not smitten before your enemies. For the Amalekites and the Canaanites are there before you, and ye shall fall by the sword: because ye are turned away from the Lord, therefore the Lord will not be with you. But they presumed to go up unto the hill top: nevertheless the ark of the covenant of the Lord, and Moses, departed not out of the camp. Then the Amalekites came down, and the Canaanites which dwelt in that hill, and smote them, and discomfited them, even unto Hormah."

Moses mentioned this incident again in his farewell speech. He reminded the people, "Then ye answered and said unto me, We have sinned against the Lord, we will go up and fight, according to all that the Lord our God commanded us. And when ye had girded on every man his weapons of war, ye were ready to go up into the hill. And the Lord said unto me, Say unto them, Go not up, neither fight; for I am not among you; lest ye be smitten before your enemies. So I spake unto you; and ye would not hear, but rebelled against the commandment of the Lord, and went presumptuously up into the hill. And the Amorites, which dwelt in that mountain, came out against you, and chased you, as bees do, and destroyed you in Seir, even unto Hormah. And ye returned and wept before the

Lord; but the Lord would not hearken to your voice, nor give ear unto you. So ye abode in Kadesh many days, according unto the days that ye abode there" (Deut. 1:41-46).

In this passage we see the Israelites praying to the Lord and confessing their sin, and yet God refused to listen to their prayers. He would not restore them to their previous situation.

Why didn't God give them success? He had already given them the Promised Land and wanted them to possess it. God did not answer their prayers and allow them to be successful because He knew their hearts were not right. He knew that their views of spiritual matters were completely inadequate. Let's look at some of these spiritual matters and notice how the people of Israel failed to understand them.

Inadequate View of Sin

The Israelites had confessed their sin, and yet God did not hear their pleas. Why did the Lord refuse to answer? Because the people had a very *inadequate view of sin*. While they said, "We have sinned," their hearts were not in their confession. Merely admitting their guilt did not make them truly repentant.

We find a number of examples in the Bible of people who also made this confession. However, while the words were the same, the meaning was not. Balaam said, "I have sinned" when he disobeyed the Lord's command, but he didn't really mean it (see Num. 22:20-34). Likewise, Pharaoh

29

said it when God was sending plagues on Egypt, but his confession was also insincere (see Ex. 9:27-35). However, others have admitted their guilt in genuine repentance. When David was confronted with his sin in killing Uriah and taking his wife, he said, "I have sinned against the Lord" (II Sam. 12:13). As the Prodigal Son returned home, he also said, "I have sinned" (Luke 15:21). In each case, the Lord examined their motives and attitudes and based His response on their hearts and actions, not their words.

While the Children of Israel were saying, "We have sinned against the Lord" (Deut. 1:41), what they said and did immediately after that seems to indicate that they were not truly repentant. They stated, "We will go up and fight" (v. 41). That word "will" bothers me. Even though the Lord told them not to attempt to conquer the land because He was not with them, they were determined to do it anyway. And, of course, they were defeated. Then they returned and cried out to God, but the Lord told them, "I am not going to pay any attention to your prayer. I am not going to hear what you are saying because your heart is not right. You don't have the right attitude, and you have an inadequate understanding of sin."

What was the Israelites' sin? First, they committed the sin of unbelief. They did not believe God when He said, "Go in and take the land." This sin led to another sin—disobedience. They refused to go into Canaan. Third, they were guilty of murmuring. They complained, "Let's go back to Egypt. Why should we die here in the wilderness?" (see Num. 14:3,4). Because of their murmuring and disobedience, Moses told them, "You have passed your own sentence. You will wander in this wilderness until every person 20 years of age and older has died, because you have rebelled against God" (see vv. 28,29).

These sins caused the Children of Israel to despair, and despair led to more presumption. They said, "We are sorry for what we have done. We will go up and take the land as God told us to before" (see vv. 40-45). However, they had no idea of the gravity of their sin. They thought they could just tell God they were sorry and that would be the end of it. They believed that He would then help them conquer the land. However, the Israelites had an inadequate view of sin. They had robbed God of His glory and had disobeyed His express will; therefore, He would not listen to their prayer.

Like the Israelites, we often don't see sin for what it really is. If we realized just how serious the sins of disobedience, rebellion and unbelief really are, we would flee from them. God warns us that if we possess an evil heart of unbelief, our end will be the same as for the Children of Israel in the wilderness (see Heb. 3:7—4:1).

Inadequate View of God's Pardon

Not only did the Israelites have an inadequate view of their sin, but they also had an *inadequate view of God's pardon*. Even though they had to suffer the consequences of their sin, the Lord forgave them for their unbelief and disobedience. Numbers 14:20 tells us, "And the Lord said, I have pardoned according to thy word." However, the people didn't appreciate the forgiveness they had received. All they could see was the punishment they had been given in not being able to enter the Promised Land.

In the preceding verses, we discover that God pardoned the people's sin, not for their sake but for Moses' sake. Because of His great anger at their sin, the Lord was ready to slay the whole nation and start over again with Moses and his descendants, as He had done in the days of Noah. Moses pleaded with God to spare the people, arguing that the other nations would say that He didn't have the power to bring His people into the land (see vv. 13-16). God listened to Moses' prayer and pardoned the people for his sake (not because the people deserved it), allowing their children to enter the land 40 years later.

In Moses' plea for the people, we discover an important truth about God's forgiveness. Moses stated, "The Lord is longsuffering, and of great mercy, forgiving iniquity and transgression, and by no means clearing the guilty, visiting the iniquity of the fathers upon the children unto the third and fourth generation" (v. 18). Our God is indeed patient and merciful. He will forgive us when we come to Him in true repentance. However, this does not mean that He will remove the results of our sin. Often we, and even our children and grand-

children, must bear the natural and painful consequences of what we have done.

Because the Children of Israel were looking at the
results of their sin, they did not appreciate the pardon they had received. God's pardon should have
led these people to a deeper sense of commitment
and obedience. Psalm 130:4 says, "But there is forgiveness with thee, that thou mayest be feared."
When people really understand God's pardon,
realizing that forgiveness is not cheap, it leads them
to a deeper respect for the Lord.

Inadequate View of Repentance

Because the Israelites did not see the gravity of
their sin or the greatness of God's pardon, they had
a very *inadequate view of repentance.* In reality, the
people did not really repent at all. Instead, they
merely experienced a sense of regret and remorse.

In II Corinthians 7:10, Paul described the difference between remorse and repentance when he
stated, "For godly sorrow worketh repentance to
salvation not to be repented of: but the sorrow of
the world worketh death." The Children of Israel
were feeling great remorse and regret for what they
had done because of its worldly results—not
because they had sinned against God. They regret-
ted their sin because it meant that they would not be
able to enter the land but would die in the wilderness. They were not concerned about the character
of their hearts; they were concerned only about the
consequences of their acts. They admitted their

guilt only because they hoped it would enable them to avoid the consequences.

Dr. William Culbertson, the late president of the Moody Bible Institute, often talked about the "consequences of forgiven sin." While God, in His grace, pardons us when we repent of our sin, God, in His government, says to us, "You shall reap what you've sown." Real repentance leads to submission to God's will and acceptance of the results of our sin. While the Israelites admitted they had sinned, the fact that they were unwilling to accept God's judgment shows they had not truly repented. Instead of submitting to God in humble obedience, they disobeyed His direct command not to fight the Amalekites and Canaanites (see Num. 14:39-45).

Inadequate View of Prayer

In addition, the Children of Israel had a very *inadequate view of prayer*. They believed that they could change God's mind through prayer. After all, they reasoned, Moses had prayed on previous occasions, and God had relented (or so it appeared). But the purpose of prayer is not to change God's mind. It is to discover His will. In order for prayer to be effective, it must go hand in hand with the Word of God. "If ye abide in me, and my words abide in you, ye shall ask what ye will, and it shall be done unto you" (John 15:7). The people had rejected God's word and disobeyed His commands; therefore, the Lord would not respond to their prayers.

In Zechariah 7:12,13 we find an interesting statement about the link between prayer and the Word of God: "Yea, they made their hearts as an adamant stone, lest they should hear the law, and the words which the Lord of hosts hath sent in his spirit by the former prophets: therefore came a great wrath from the Lord of hosts. Therefore it is come to pass, that as he cried, and they would not hear; so they cried, and I would not hear, saith the Lord of hosts." In this passage God is saying, "You cried out, and I didn't hear you. You want to know why? It's because when I cried out, you wouldn't listen to Me." These verses have grave implications for believers today. God treats us the way we treat Him. If we become hard and callous, refusing to listen to and obey God's Word, then the Lord will turn a deaf ear to our prayers for help.

Inadequate View of God's Will

The Israelites had a very inadequate view of sin, of God's pardon, of repentance and of prayer. At the root of these misconceptions was their *inadequate view of the will of God*. The people didn't realize that God's will involves not only *what* should be done but also *who* should do it, *how* it should be done, *why* it should be done and *when* it should be done. God had told the Israelites, "It is My will that you go into the Promised Land. You will be led by Joshua. You will possess the land by My power and do it for My glory. I don't want you to wait but want you to go immediately and conquer the land, relying on My guidance and power." However, the people didn't follow God's instructions. They ignored His will and followed their own plans. While they

35

wanted to enter the land, they desired to do it their way and in their time.

We find an interesting statement regarding God's timing in Hebrews 4:1: "Let us therefore fear, lest, a promise being left us of entering into his rest, any of you should seem to come short of it." The Greek word that is translated "come short" is a military term that means "to arrive late" or "to fall behind." It's a picture of a soldier marching out of step, falling behind the rest of the army. Thus, this verse could be rendered, "Let us therefore fear, lest, a promise being left us of entering into his rest, any of you should [arrive too late]."

This is exactly what happened to the Israelites. They came a day late. The previous day, when they received the spies report, they could have entered the land if they had believed God. However, because they doubted His power and His will, they waited. The next day they realized that they had been wrong, but by then it was too late. They had fallen behind God's timing and thus missed entering into the rest He had prepared for them.

Don't play games with the will of God. The Lord hates presumption, false confidence and self-will. The Israelites presumed that because they had admitted their sins, God would still help them conquer the land. Even when Moses warned them that God would not help them, they stubbornly followed their own will and confidently marched off to fight the enemy. As a result, they were soundly defeated.

Likewise, we must not assume that God will always help us, even when we are out of His will and plan. George MacDonald said, "In whatever man does without God, he must fail miserably—or succeed more miserably." While we fail often because we are not following God's will, sometimes the Lord allows us to succeed in our presumption and in our self-will; however, we always regret it. In the case of the Israelites, God said, "You are not going to succeed." And they did indeed fail miserably.

The Lord is often forced to discipline us. When we have trifled with God's will, we tend to cry out, "Oh, God, put it back the way it was before!" At these times, God must reply, "I can't do that." As in the case of the Children of Israel, God must often start over again with a new generation. This often happens in our churches and our ministries. Sometimes we come to our Kadesh-barnea and simply need to enter in by faith and claim what God has for us. But instead of stepping out in faith, we back off. Then, after we have waited too long, we presumptuously try to go ahead with God's original plan. However, the Lord must say to us, "No, I'm sorry, but I can't bless you now."

This is why it is so important for us to obey God when He tells us to obey Him. "Now is the accepted time; behold, now is the day of salvation" (II Cor. 6:2). If God is speaking to you about doing something, do it. Don't lag behind the will of God.

God, in His grace, pardons us when we realize the seriousness of our sin and come to Him in an attitude of genuine repentance and submission. However, God, in His government, disciplines in love when His children disobey. He permits our

37

stubbornness to bring about its consequences. Thus, it is vital that we understand the purpose of prayer and honestly seek His will. As God's children, we must not only do the will of God but also do the will of God *on time*.

Chapter 4

The Prophet Who Wanted to Die

(I Kings 19:1-14)

Elijah the prophet wanted to die. He asked God to take his life because he had come to the conclusion that he was a failure. Elijah had just been victorious in the showdown with the 450 prophets of Baal on Mount Carmel. God had sent fire down from heaven to consume Elijah's sacrifice (see I Kings 18:17-40). In addition, the prophet had predicted a terrible famine, and the Lord had not sent rain for three years. After that time, Elijah prayed for rain, and God produced a torrential downpour (see vv. 41-46).

God was working mightily through His servant Elijah. This made him very unpopular with Ahab and Jezebel, the wicked king and queen of Israel. We read in I Kings 19:1-3: "And Ahab told Jezebel all that Elijah had done, and withal how he had slain all the prophets with the sword. Then Jezebel sent a messenger unto Elijah, saying, So let the gods do to me, and more also, if I make not thy life as the life of one of them by to morrow about this time. And when he saw that, he arose, and went for his life, and came to Beer-sheba, which belongeth to Judah, and left his servant there."

When Elijah heard Jezebel's death threat, he fled for his life. He traveled about 100 miles from Jezreel down to Beer-sheba, located along the outer border of Israel. Considering all the powerful works the Lord had just performed through Elijah, it is hard to understand why the prophet didn't stay and face Jezebel, trusting God to protect him. Instead, he fled into the wilderness and requested to die.

"But he himself went a day's journey into the wilderness, and came and sat down under a juniper tree: and he requested for himself that he might die; and said, It is enough; now, O Lord, take away my life; for I am not better than my fathers. And as he lay and slept under a juniper tree, behold, then an angel touched him, and said unto him, Arise and eat. And he looked, and, behold, there was a cake baken on the coals, and a cruse of water at his head. And he did eat and drink, and laid him down again. And the angel of the Lord came again the second time, and touched him, and said, Arise and eat; because the journey is too great for thee. And he arose, and did eat and drink, and went in the strength of that meat forty days and forty nights unto Horeb the mount of God.

"And he came thither unto a cave, and lodged there; and, behold, the word of the Lord came to him, and he said unto him, What doest thou here, Elijah? And he said, I have been very jealous for the Lord God of hosts: for the children of Israel have forsaken thy covenant, thrown down thine altars, and slain thy prophets with the sword; and I, even I only, am left; and they seek my life, to take it away. And he said, Go forth, and stand upon the mount before the Lord. And, behold, the Lord passed by, and a great and strong wind rent the mountains, and brake in pieces the rocks before the Lord; but the Lord was not in the wind: and after the wind an earthquake; but the Lord was not in the earthquake: and after the earthquake a fire; but the Lord was not in the fire: and after the fire a still small voice. And it was so, when Elijah heard it, that he wrapped his face in his mantle, and went out, and stood in the entering in of the cave. And, behold, there came a voice unto him, and said, What doest thou here, Elijah? And he said, I have been very jealous for the Lord God of hosts: because the children of Israel have forsaken thy covenant, thrown down thine altars, and slain thy prophets with the sword; and I, even I only, am left; and they seek my life, to take it away" (vv. 4-14).

Elijah had quite an experience, didn't he? He was terribly discouraged. He had remained faithful in proclaiming God's message, yet the only result, as far as he could see, was a threat on his life. He believed that he was the only faithful person left. Like so many other great leaders, Elijah requested that he be allowed to die rather than go on as he had been. When his burden had seemed too great to carry, Moses had also asked God to take his life (see Num. 11:11-15). Likewise, Jonah preferred to die rather than watch the Ninevites repent and be

41

spared by God (see Jon. 4:3). Jeremiah cursed the day of his birth (see Jer. 20:14-18), as did Job (see Job 3:1-16). These were all great men of God, yet even at their greatest, they were still men. James 5:17 tells us that Elijah possessed the same nature (one that is subject to the same emotions) as we have.

These examples should be a reminder to us never to place any preacher or Christian worker on a pedestal. If we do, we should always make sure we look at their feet—not their face. When we do, we'll find that they also have feet of clay. Every man at his best is still a man. They will fail. Some of the greatest people in the Bible failed in their strongest points. Moses, the meek and humble servant, became proud and boastful. Abraham, the great man of faith, doubted God and lied about his wife. Peter, a courageous man, became fearful and denied the Lord three times. Realizing that our leaders are not perfect will enable us to better understand and help them in their ministry.

When he became depressed and discouraged, Elijah reacted as most people do—he sought release from his troubles through death. However, God refused to answer his prayer. Instead, the Lord provided the physical nourishment and spiritual encouragement that he needed to go on. Why did God choose not to answer Elijah's prayer? In this passage we find several important factors that help us understand why God responded as He did. The Lord evaluates our prayers in the same manner in determining whether or not to answer them.

42

God Looked Behind Him

When Elijah requested to die, *God first looked behind him* and saw what he had just been through. Elijah's confrontation with the prophets of Baal on Mount Carmel had been spiritually, physically and emotionally demanding on him. His life had been in danger. He was tired. His nerves had been stretched to the breaking point. Emotionally and physically, he was not at his best.

We all know that when we are tired, hungry and emotionally drained, we become discouraged. In this mental state, we often say things we don't really mean. The Lord understands our human nature. He loves us and knows what is best for us—even when we don't. Psalm 103 tells us, "Like as a father pitieth his children, so the Lord pitieth them that fear him. For he knoweth our frame; he remembereth that we are dust" (vv. 13,14). God takes our human nature, with its problems, into account when considering our requests. He often refuses to give us what we ask for, knowing that it is not the best solution.

The Lord looked back at the recent events in Elijah's life and realized that his request was motivated by his physical, mental and emotional exhaustion—not by a genuine desire to die. Thus, God did not answer Elijah's prayer. Instead, He gave the prophet what he really needed. The Lord sent an angel to minister to his physical needs, providing food and water. Then God directed Elijah to Mount Horeb, where He reminded the prophet of His great power. This renewed Elijah's faith and spiritual strength and prepared him to go back and face his enemies (see I Kings 19:15-19).

God Looked Within Him

God not only looked behind Elijah and saw what he had been through, but also *He looked within Elijah* and saw that the real problem was in his heart. Elijah's heart was filled with unbelief. When he received the message that Jezebel was going to kill him, he fled to the wilderness and cried out, "Lord, take my life."

Obviously, Elijah didn't really want to die. If he had, he would have stayed where he was and let Jezebel take care of it! Likewise, I don't think Jezebel really wanted to kill Elijah. She threatened him in an effort to frighten him off. Elijah had just won a great victory against the false prophets of Baal. When the people had seen God's power in consuming the sacrifice, they had cried out, "The Lord, he is the God" (I Kings 18:39). Jezebel feared that Elijah would start a great revival, preaching to the people and leading them back to God. By running away, Elijah gave Jezebel exactly what she wanted.

Elijah was walking by sight, not by faith. When Jezebel heard about everything the prophet had done, she said, "I will take care of you" (see 19:2). We then read in the next verse: "And when he saw that, he arose and went for his life" (v. 3). Instead of trusting God to take care of him, Elijah looked at the circumstances and ran in fear.

Prior to this incident, we find that whenever God wanted Elijah to do something, the prophet had always heard and obeyed the word of the Lord. We read in I Kings 17:2,3: "And the word of the Lord came unto him, saying, Get thee hence, and turn thee eastward, and hide thyself by the brook Cherith, that is before Jordan." Likewise, we later read: "And the word of the Lord came unto him, saying, Arise, get thee to Zarephath" (vv. 8,9). Later, when God told the prophet to appear before Ahab, he immediately did it, even though he knew that his life would be in danger (see 18:1,2).

However, Satan began to work in the area of Elijah's strength—his unswerving obedience to God's word—and caused him to begin to doubt and become impatient. He ran ahead of God rather than waiting for the Lord to reveal His will to him. Isaiah 28:16 tells us, "He that believeth shall not make haste."

Elijah also had a heart of pride. He stated, "O Lord, take away my life; for I am not better than my fathers" (I Kings 19:4). The prophet seemed to be more concerned about his reputation than he was about his ministry. In addition, self-pity moved in. Elijah felt sorry for himself. He had worked so hard, but all he had received in return was hatred. So he decided to protect himself instead of doing the work of God. However, Jesus stated, "He that saves his life shall lose it, but he that loses his life for My sake shall find it" (see Matt. 10:39).

Instead of trusting God and staying to face Jezebel, Elijah fled to the wilderness, where he wal-

45

lowed in self-pity. He was discouraged and alone. When you are very discouraged, you should never spend a lot of time alone. It only breeds more depression and self-pity. Elijah should have taken his servant with him rather than leaving him in Beer-sheba.

In the wilderness God instructed Elijah to meet Him on Mount Horeb, located about 200 miles away. This is the same place Moses had talked with God. It took Elijah 40 days to travel there. Normally the trip didn't take that long; thus, Elijah must have wandered around in the wilderness for some time, sulking and disobeying God's orders to go. But the Lord didn't say a word to Elijah as he wandered. However, on Mount Horeb, God told the prophet, in effect, "Elijah, the whole problem is you have your eyes on people. You don't have your eyes on Me."

Like Elijah, pastors often become discouraged and weary. The worst time in the world for you to come to your pastor with some criticism is right after he has preached. This is the time when he is the most tired and his nerves are strained. He needs the special rest that only God can give him. Don't criticize your pastor after he has preached, for he is very vulnerable after he has had a tremendous time of sharing God's Word. Wait until he is rested and refreshed.

God looked within Elijah and saw a heart filled with unbelief, impatience, pride and self-pity. He saw that Elijah was walking by sight, not by faith. The prophet had his eyes on Jezebel, on the backsliders in Israel and on himself instead of on the Lord. Thus, Elijah was praying with wrong motives and perceptions. He needed a change of heart—not an end to his life.

God Looked Beyond Him

The Lord had yet another reason for not answering Elijah's prayer. God not only looked behind him and saw what he had gone through and looked within him and saw his spiritual condition, but also *He looked beyond him* and saw what He had planned for him.

What if God had chosen to answer Elijah's prayer? What if the Lord had said, "Very well, Elijah, I will let you die. Just lie down in the wilderness and wait for Me to take you"? Elijah would have missed God's wonderful plan for his life. The Lord had planned that Elijah would never die. Instead, a chariot of fire appeared, and Elijah was taken up to heaven in a whirlwind (see II Kings 2:11). Throughout history, Elijah has been remembered as one of God's greatest prophets. He was later given the privilege of being with Jesus Christ and Moses on the Mount of Transfiguration (see Matt. 17:1-3). If God had answered Elijah's prayer, he would have died a defeated man. But instead, the Lord looked ahead and told Elijah, "Don't give up! I have something even better planned for you. Trust Me, and I will give you glory and honor."

Even when we appear to be praying within the Lord's will, God often does not answer our prayers because He has something even better in mind for

47

us. When I look back at my life and ministry, I can see how God was often gracious to me by not answering my prayers. I was praying for certain things I felt I needed and certain events I thought had to take place, but God said, "I'm not going to give you what you want. Let Me give you something better." The Lord knows what is best for us.

God's Response to What He Saw

The Lord looked behind, beyond and within Elijah and determined that his prayer was not in his best interest. But even though God refused to answer the prophet's prayer, He did not leave him alone and helpless. The Lord gave Elijah just what he needed to put his life together again.

What did God do for His servant? He realized, first of all, that Elijah was tired and hungry, and so He *refreshed* him (see I Kings 19:5-7). While Elijah slept under a juniper tree, the Lord sent an angel to prepare a meal for the prophet. When the angel awakened Elijah, he found a cake and a jar of water waiting for him. Having slept and eaten twice, Elijah was physically refreshed and renewed. This enabled him to have a more positive outlook on life.

As God's people, we often spend so much time and energy serving Him that we neglect our needs. When we become physically, mentally and emotionally exhausted, we cannot give our best to Him. We also tend to become discouraged and unhappy. At these times, the most spiritual thing we can do is rest. Our bodies are the temple of the Holy Spirit

48

(see I Cor. 3:16); therefore, God expects us to take care of them.

After Elijah had been refreshed, God sent him to Mount Horeb. On the mountain, the Lord appeared to the prophet. He asked Elijah what he was doing there, and the prophet complained that he was the only person left who was following Him (see I Kings 19:9,10). God then *reminded* Elijah of His great power and *rebuked* him for his lack of faith.

As Elijah stood on the mountain, God sent a terrible wind (possibly a tornado) that ripped apart the rocks. Then the ground began to shake with a violent earthquake. This was followed by a raging fire. During this magnificent display of His power, the Lord remained silent. Then, when all was quiet again, God spoke to Elijah in a still, small voice (see vv. 11-13). He said, in effect, "Elijah, while I have the power to perform great miracles, it is My word that changes people. You are looking for instant success and miracles. You want the whole nation to turn to Me. Stop looking at yourself. Stop measuring your ministry by your standards. This only leads to discouragement. Trust Me and My plan. Go back where you belong and start preaching My message. And, remember, you are not alone. I have 7000 people in Israel who are still true to Me."

After Elijah had been physically and mentally refreshed and had been rebuked by God in order to renew him spiritually, the Lord *recommissioned* him. He sent the prophet back to the battlefield. God made Elijah walk that 300-mile trip from Mount Horeb back to Beer-sheba and then to Jezreel.

Elijah had wandered away from God's chosen path for him. So he had to retrace his steps in order to get back to where the Lord wanted him.

But God did not send Elijah back alone. The Lord provided someone who helped Elijah during the remainder of his ministry and who *replaced* him when he was gone. God instructed Elijah to anoint Elisha as His prophet (see vv. 16,19-21).

When it appears that God is not answering your prayers, remember, He knows your heart. He knows what you have been through in the past and what lies ahead of you in the future. He knows what is best for you. Trust the Lord and wait patiently for His will to be revealed, realizing that He may have something even better planned for you than what you have requested of Him.

Chapter 5

A Graveyard Prayer Meeting
(Luke 8:26-40)

The Bible records some unusual prayer meetings. Jonah prayed to the Lord from the belly of the great fish (see Jon. 2:1). Daniel was thrown in the lion's den for praying to God, where he no doubt prayed during the long night (see Dan. 6:4-24). During a terrible storm at sea, Paul prayed while on board the ship and later while swimming to shore (see Acts 27:14-44). In addition, Paul often prayed when he was in prison.

However, one of the strangest prayer meetings ever recorded in Scripture took place when the Lord Jesus traveled to the area of the Gadarenes (or Gerasenes). We read in Luke 8:26-40: "And they arrived at the country of the Gadarenes, which is over against Galilee. And when he went forth to land, there met him out of the city a certain man, which had devils long time, and ware no clothes, neither abode in any house, but in the tombs. When he saw Jesus, he cried out, and fell down before him, and with a loud voice said, What have I to do

51

with thee, Jesus, thou Son of God most high? I beseech thee, torment me not. (For he had commanded the unclean spirit to come out of the man. For oftentimes it had caught him: and he was kept bound with chains and in fetters; and he brake the bands, and was driven of the devil into the wilderness.) And Jesus asked him, saying, What is thy name? And he said, Legion: because many devils were entered into him. And they besought him that he would not command them to go out into the deep [the abyss; the place of punishment]. And there was there an herd of many swine feeding on the mountain: and they besought him that he would suffer them to enter into them. And he suffered them. Then went the devils out of the man, and entered into the swine: and the herd ran violently down a steep place into the lake, and were choked [drowned].

"When they that fed them saw what was done, they fled, and went and told it in the city and in the country. Then they went out to see what was done; and came to Jesus, and found the man, out of whom the devils were departed, sitting at the feet of Jesus, clothed, and in his right mind: and they were afraid. They also which saw it told them by what means he that was possessed of the devils was healed. Then the whole multitude of the country of the Gadarenes round about besought him to depart from them; for they were taken with great fear: and he went up into the ship, and returned back again.

"Now the man out of whom the devils were departed besought him that he might be with him:

but Jesus sent him away, saying, Return to thine own house, and shew how great things God hath done unto thee. And he went his way, and published throughout the whole city how great things Jesus had done unto him. And it came to pass, that, when Jesus was returned, the people gladly received him: for they were all waiting for him."

In this exciting story we notice three different prayers that were uttered. First, the demons prayed that the Lord would not send them to the place of punishment but would allow them to enter the herd of swine instead (see vv. 31,32). The second prayer was that of the citizens, who fearfully begged Jesus to leave the area (see v. 37). Then the man who had been delivered from the demons prayed that he might have the privilege of going with Jesus and becoming one of His disciples (see v. 38). Interestingly enough, the Lord Jesus answered the prayers of the demons and the unbelieving citizens, but He did not answer the prayer of the man who had been delivered. Let's examine the motives behind Christ's response to these prayers.

The Prayer of the Demons

In this passage, we see Christ responding first to *the prayer of the demons*. As Jesus and His disciples landed on the shores of the region of Gadara, they saw a demon-possessed man wandering through the burial grounds outside the city. When the disheveled and unclothed man saw the Lord Jesus, the demons inside him immediately cried out,

"What have I to do with thee, Jesus, thou Son of God most high?" (Luke 8:28).

It is interesting to note that in every instance where Christ encountered demons, these spirits always acknowledged who He was—the holy Son of God. In this respect, the demons are smarter than some liberals today. Many liberal theologians do not believe that Jesus is the Son of God, but the demons know who He is. They recognize His great power and tremble in His presence. James 2:19 tells us, "Thou believest that there is one God; thou doest well: the devils also believe, and tremble." While the knowledge of who Christ is should cause us to stand in awe and fear before His wonderful presence, mere knowledge of Him is not enough. We must commit our lives to the Lord in complete obedience to His will. Otherwise, we are no different from the demons.

While many have tried to explain away demon possession, saying that this man was merely mentally disturbed, the demons were very real. They had robbed this man of everything worthwhile in life. A host of evil spirits had taken over his life, stealing his health, his sanity, his morality and his decency. They were destroying his mind and body, robbing him of his peace. This is what Satan does to those who allow him to gain control. He is a destroyer and a thief. In describing the Devil, Jesus stated, "The thief cometh not, but for to steal, and to kill, and to destroy: I am come that they might have life, and that they might have it more abundantly" (John 10:10).

While Satan is able to control and destroy lives, he and his demons are powerless in the presence of the Lord Jesus. Notice that the demons never questioned the fact that they would be cast out. Once Jesus had come to give this man life, they were powerless to resist His will. This account teaches us several valuable lessons. First, we see that the demons believed in the deity of Jesus Christ and the reality of hell. They also believed in the power of prayer, begging the Lord not to send them into the abyss (see Luke 8:31). If Satan and his demons believe these important truths, how much more should we believe them! Second, while Satan is able to control us when we let him, we need to remember that Christ's power is even greater. When we allow the Lord to rule in our hearts, the Devil will flee in terror.

The Prayer of the Citizens

Not only did Jesus answer the prayer of the demons, permitting them to enter the herd of swine, but He also answered *the prayer of the citizens*, who begged Jesus to leave their region (see Luke 8:37).

Once the demons had been allowed to enter the swine, the poor, crazed animals raced madly over a cliff and drowned in the sea below. Seeing this, the excited and frightened herders rushed back to the city to spread the news. While it is not certain who these people were, it is generally believed that they were Gentiles. Because of the prohibitions against

55

eating pork and handling unclean animals, it is doubtful that a group of Jewish people would have owned such a herd. When the citizens heard what had happened, they hurried out to see for themselves.

Upon their arrival, the crowd discovered that the herd had indeed been destroyed. However, they also saw the former demoniac—fully clothed and sitting calmly at the feet of Jesus. What a change from his old life! When the people saw what Jesus had done for the man, they should have rejoiced. This man had been the terror of the neighborhood for a long time. He had not one demon—but an entire legion of demons. This is a reference to a Roman legion, which had as many as 6000 soldiers in it. He had been running around the city naked, screaming and cutting himself. He had been frightening the children. The citizens had tried to chain him, but he had broken the fetters. Then they had isolated and threatened him, but these, too, had not solved the problem. They should have been grateful to Jesus for solving their dilemma. In fact, it should be noted that Matthew mentioned *two* demoniacs (see Matt. 8:28). No doubt Jesus healed both of them, so the citizens should have been doubly grateful.

But instead of gratitude, the people displayed an attitude of fear, anger and alarm. They were angry and alarmed at the destruction of the herd. The Lord had wrecked the economy of the city. They were afraid of what He might do next. It is interesting that they did not appear to be afraid when the man had been a dangerous demoniac. They had becomed accustomed to that. However, they were frightened at the change that had taken place in him. Jesus had forgiven the man and given him sanity and peace. Because the people couldn't explain this transformation, they were afraid. They wanted Jesus to leave so they did not have to face the issue.

This is often how the world reacts when confronted with the life-changing power of Christianity. I have known non-Christians who were possessed by drinking, sexual immorality and other destructive habits. They were wrecking their homes and terrorizing their families and neighborhoods. But then they were saved, and their lives underwent a dramatic transformation. They gave up their old habits and life-styles. They began attending church and reading the Bible. They were loving and kind to their families and friends. But instead of rejoicing, their relatives began to persecute them and tell them they had lost their minds. They had been more willing to accept these people when they were drinking and abusing their children. I really believe the world would rather see people wallowing in the bondage of sin than living to the glory of God.

The citizens of Gadara could not explain the transformation that had taken place in the man sitting at the feet of Jesus. Nor did they want to. If they had explained it, they would have been forced to receive it. They realized that the answer lay in Jesus, and they did not want to accept Him. This is still true today. Just as the people of His day rejected the Lord when He was on earth, so also the world today is not willing to accept Jesus Christ—or His people. Jesus realized that this would be the world's reaction to Him. He warned us, "The servant is not greater than his lord. If they have persecuted me, they will also persecute you; if they have kept my saying, they will keep your's also" (John 15:20). We can see this happening. The Lord Jesus has been pushed out of our government, our schools and many of our homes and churches. People don't want Him. It costs too much to have Him there.

Because the multitude feared what they had witnessed and were unwilling to accept Jesus Christ, they did not want the Lord to remain in their country. So they asked Him to leave. Jesus granted their request. He and the disciples climbed back into the boat and left (see Luke 8:37). It is interesting to see the contrast between the two crowds. The citizens of Gadara couldn't wait for Jesus to leave, while the people to whom He returned gladly welcomed Him.

Why did Jesus answer the prayer of the unbelieving citizens? Because He will not force Himself on anyone. Even though Christ has all power and desires that everyone be saved (see II Pet. 3:9), He does not make anyone accept His will. Jesus is standing at the door and knocking (see Rev. 3:20). If we refuse to answer the door, He will eventually depart. Tragically, the day comes when people want to call on Him, but because they have asked Him to leave, He is no longer there to hear them. This is why it is vital to "seek ye the Lord while he may be found, call ye upon him while he is near" (Isa. 55:6).

The Prayer of the New Believer

Christ answered the prayer of the demons and of the citizens of Gadara, yet we find that He did not answer *the prayer of the new believer* from whom He had cast out the legion of demons.

When the man had been released from the bondage of demon possession, his natural reaction was one of extreme gratitude and happiness. He wanted to be with Jesus and learn more from Him (see Luke 8:38). This was a logical prayer. In addition, the Lord and His disciples had endured hardships in order to save this man. Therefore, it would be natural for Jesus to want this man to join them. They had braved a terrible storm at sea in which Jesus had calmed the angry waves—and the frightened disciples (see vv. 22-25). When they landed on shore, they encountered the naked, screaming, dangerous demoniac. This man could have attacked and harmed Jesus and the disciples. The Lord courageously faced the wild man and commanded the demons to depart from him. Once the demons left him, the man became a different person because of his relationship with Christ (see II Cor. 5:17).

This raises the question: Since this man was a new creature in Christ, why didn't the Lord answer his prayer? Jesus refused to allow the man to come with Him but instead sent him away, saying, "Return to thine own house, and shew how great things God hath done unto thee" (Luke 8:39).

Christian Living Begins at Home

In this passage I find two reasons why Jesus chose not to answer the man's prayer. First, *Christian living begins at home.*

I recall an incident that took place in one of the churches I pastored. A man phoned me, wanting to meet for lunch. He had recently come to Christ through the ministry of a good friend of mine. During lunch, the man asked me, "Now that I'm a Christian, what should I do next?"

I replied, "Well, what about your family?"

"Well," he answered, "my wife is not a Christian."

"Then you should go home and start witnessing to her. You should also begin going to the church where you found the Lord as your Saviour and give God a chance to work in your home."

However, the man chose not to follow my advice. He decided that he wanted to become involved in Christian service. So he started an organization and began traveling around the country, preaching and singing. It wasn't long before his home fell apart. Christian living doesn't begin on the mission field—it begins at home.

The former demoniac was excited about his new life in Christ and immediately wanted to become one of the Lord's disciples. However, Christ realized that he had unfinished work at home to complete. Jesus told him, "No, you can't come with Me. It is much more important for you to return home and tell your family and others what great things God has done for you. This is your first responsibility."

Christian Work Begins With Witness

The second reason why the Lord did not answer the man's prayer is because *Christian work begins with witness.* What most of us do not realize is that being a worker for Christ and being a witness for Him are not necessarily the same thing. While God has given every Christian some gift that can be used for the good of others and for His glory, the Lord does not call every believer into Christian work per se. However, every Christian is called to be a witness (see Luke 24:46-48; Acts 1:8). We have many people in our churches today who are church workers, yet they are not witnesses. They have never really told someone else about what Christ has done for them. However, the Lord says to us, "Before I call you as a worker, I want you to be a witness."

We discover another important truth as well. When Jesus was on earth in a human body, He had limitations. He could not be everywhere at once. Thus, Jesus told the former demoniac, in effect, "Look, I can't go to your home. I must go back to where I came from, but you are going to represent Me. I want you to take My place and tell the people what I have done for you."

This is also true today. While Jesus is no longer limited, He has chosen to work through His followers rather than doing the job Himself. He has told us, "As my Father hath sent me, even so send I you" (John 20:21). The basis for all Christian work is witness. Telling others about Christ should be our first priority, because if we don't do it, the job will not get done.

Notice the man's reaction to Christ's refusal. He did not balk or complain but immediately went his way and published throughout the whole city the great things Jesus had done for him. We know that sometimes the hardest place to take a stand for Christ is among our friends and relatives. However, this man was not ashamed to tell others about Him. We do not know how the people responded to his witness, but no doubt some people accepted the Lord.

This incident teaches us not only the importance of witness and service at home but of the Lord's purposes in answering, or not answering, our prayers. While the demons and the citizens did not deserve to have their prayers answered, the Lord chose to grant them their requests in order to achieve a greater end. While Jesus could have sent the demons into the abyss, He allowed them to enter the swine as a dramatic demonstration to the people. Likewise, Christ chose to depart as the people requested in order to minister to those who wanted Him and to give the healed demoniac the opportunity to witness to them. And even though the former demoniac's request was honorable, the Lord did not answer it because He had another purpose in mind for the new believer. By fulfilling his responsibility to witness at home, the man grew in his faith and brought greater glory to God.

Often the Lord has purposes in mind that we are not aware of. He may refuse to answer our prayers because to do so would thwart His ultimate plan. If the Lord has not answered our prayers to be used by Him in His work, it could be that we have some unfinished work and witness at home. Whatever the reason for His refusals, we should trust Christ and accept His denials, even if we cannot see the purpose behind these unanswered prayers. He may choose to reveal His will to us in time. Even if He doesn't, we know that ultimately God will be glorified, and that is enough.

Chapter 6

A Prayer From Beyond the Grave
(Luke 16:19-31)

Throughout the Gospels, Christ emphasized the proper attitude toward, and use of, money. In Luke 16 we find a twofold message concerning the resources that have been entrusted to us.

The Lord began His teaching in this chapter with the parable of the unjust steward (see vv. 1-13). While Jesus did not condone the actions of the unjust steward in cheating his employer, He did commend him for the way he made use of his opportunity to provide for himself after he had been fired. Christ's message in this parable was this: *Make the most of your opportunities.*

Jesus followed this parable with the story of the rich man and Lazarus. While many consider this story to be a parable, I believe that it was an actual account. In this account, Jesus built on His previous message. Not only are we to make use of our opportunities, but we should also *make wise and proper use of our wealth for His service.* In the first parable, the unjust steward made friends through the use of his money. Christ then used the second account to make a spiritual application. He said, in effect, "Make friends by means of your money so that when you enter heaven, they will be waiting for you. Use your money and your opportunities now to serve God."

In the narrative of the rich man and Lazarus, the Lord related the life story of a man who wasted the wealth and opportunities God had given him. He used them entirely for his own pleasure, never helping anyone in need. As a result, the rich man suffered eternal torment. We read: "There was a certain rich man, which was clothed in purple and fine linen, and fared sumptuously every day: and there was a certain beggar named Lazarus, which was laid at his gate, full of sores, and desiring to be fed with the crumbs which fell from the rich man's table: moreover the dogs came and licked his sores.

"And it came to pass, that the beggar died, and was carried by the angels into Abraham's bosom: the rich man also died, and was buried; and in hell [hades] he lift up his eyes, being in torments, and seeth Abraham afar off, and Lazarus in his bosom. And he cried and said, Father Abraham, have mercy on me, and send Lazarus, that he may dip the tip of his finger in water, and cool my tongue; for I am tormented in this flame. But Abraham said, Son, remember that thou in thy lifetime receivedst thy good things, and likewise Lazarus evil things: but now he is comforted, and thou art tormented. And beside all this, between us and you there is a great gulf fixed: so that they which would pass from hence to you cannot; neither can they pass to us, that would come from thence.

"Then he said, I pray thee therefore, father, that thou wouldest send him to my father's house: for I have five brethren; that he may testify unto them, lest they also come into this place of torment. Abraham saith unto him, They have Moses and the prophets; let them hear them. And he said, Nay, father Abraham: but if one went unto them from the dead, they will repent. And he said unto him, If they hear not Moses and the prophets, neither will they be persuaded, though one rose from the dead" (vv. 19-31).

While we can learn much from this passage regarding the importance of using our money and opportunities for the Lord while on earth, I believe that this account teaches us an important lesson about prayer as well. In this story, the Lord Jesus Christ lifted the veil between life and death, between time and eternity, and gave us a glimpse into the afterlife. As we look, we see two men. Lazarus, a poor, diseased beggar while on earth, has died and been taken to Abraham's bosom (paradise) where he awaits his eternal rewards in heaven. A rich man dies shortly thereafter and finds himself in hades, a place of torment for those awaiting eternal punishment in hell. The suffering rich man cries out to Abraham and Lazarus, uttering two prayers—a prayer for water and a prayer for witness. Neither of these prayers was answered by the Lord. In this passage we discover three reasons why the rich man's prayers went unanswered.

He Prayed in the Wrong Place

The first reason why the rich man's prayers were unheeded was because *he prayed in the wrong place.* Luke 16:23 tells us, "And in hell [hades] he lifted up his eyes."

While the King James Version and other English translations render this "hell," the word used in the original Greek is "hades," a temporary place of punishment where unbelievers go after they die. By contrast, hell is the permanent abode of the unsaved. On the Day of Judgment, both the living and the dead who have not accepted Christ will be cast into hell for eternity. "It is appointed unto men once to die, but after this the judgment" (Heb. 9:27).

The fact that hades and hell are two distinct places is even more evident in Revelation 20, where we read that at the final judgment the dead will be brought up from death and hades and will be cast into the lake of fire (see vv. 13,14). Thus, hades and the lake of fire are not the same. The word "death" here refers to the grave. While the grave claims a person's body at death, hades claims his soul and spirit. Following the Judgment, the unbeliever's body, soul and spirit will once again be united and will be cast into hell (the lake of fire).

Thus, we see that, at death, the rich man's soul and spirit were transported to hades to await the Judgment. Why was he in that place? The reason

67

was not because he was rich. Abraham had been rich on earth. The difference between these two men lay in their hearts. Abraham was a great man of faith, who trusted and served God continually. The rich man, on the other hand, had placed himself ahead of God. He had refused to repent. He had hardened his heart to the message of the Lord that had been sent to him through Moses and the prophets (see Luke 16:29-31). Therefore, he sealed his own fate and sent himself to this place of punishment and suffering, where he would remain until God's final verdict was rendered.

Have you ever stopped to consider just how much witness this man had received during his lifetime? Even his riches had been God's witness to him. Jesus stated that this man had "fared sumptuously" (v. 19) every day of his life. The Greek word "sumptuously" means "dazzling" or "in brilliant splendor and flamboyance." When this man saw how much the Lord had blessed him with, it should have made him feel repentant and humble, realizing that he did not deserve such blessings. Romans 2:4 tells us, "Or despisest thou the riches of his goodness and forbearance and longsuffering; not knowing that the goodness of God leadeth thee to repentance?" However, instead of repenting and allowing his splendid life to lead him to the Lord, this man let his riches come between him and God.

When we stop to reflect on the goodness of God, this knowledge should lead us to repentance. However, as in the case of the rich man, God's goodness only causes some people to harden their hearts even more. Their focus shifts from God to themselves. What is the result? "But after thy hardness and impenitent heart treasurest up unto thyself wrath against the day of wrath and revelation of the righteous judgment of God" (v. 5). When we begin looking at our material treasures and hardening our hearts against God, we are storing up for ourselves treasures of torment for eternity.

In addition to his wealth, the Lord also used Lazarus as a witness to the rich man. This beggar had sat by the rich man's gate for a long time, hoping to receive a little food from the wealthy resident (see Luke 16:20,21). Lazarus gave the rich man many opportunities to trust God and to serve Him. Obviously, the presence of this beggar could not have been ignored. However, the rich man did ignore his witness and his needs, thus missing his opportunity.

From this passage, it is evident that Lazarus had been a witness to the rich man. In hades, the rich man begged, "I pray thee therefore, father, that thou wouldest send him [Lazarus] to my father's house: for I have five brethren; that he may testify unto them, lest they also come into this place of torment" (vv. 27,28). Why did the rich man make such a request? Because Lazarus had testified to him, whether by his words or by his presence alone. When the rich man had passed the gate, Lazarus may have spoken to him, reminding him of his need to trust God. Even if Lazarus never spoke a word, his presence was a living example to the rich man that wealth and worldly possessions are fleeting;

69

therefore, he should place his faith in what is permanent—God. The rich man realized too late that Lazarus' witness had been true. He hoped to spare the rest of his family from the same fate.

Even the death of Lazarus should have been a witness to this man. Verse 22 seems to indicate that Lazarus died first. When death is at a person's doorstep, as it was at the rich man's, it often causes the person to see his need for God. However, even the death of Lazarus did not awaken the rich man to his desperate need. Then death also claimed him, and it was too late.

Not only did the rich man have the witness of his wealth and of Lazarus, but he also had the witness of the Word to tell him of his need to trust God. No doubt the man had gone to the synagogue Sabbath after Sabbath and had listened to the reading of the Law and the Prophets. However, he had not heeded the teachings. Because he ignored the testimony of the Word, of his wealth and of Lazarus, the rich man sealed his fate. Once he died and entered hades, it was too late to change his life.

In actuality, the rich man really had no desire to change his life. Death does not change a person's character. The rich man was selfish before he died; he was still selfish after his death. His prayers for water and for witness were motivated by his selfish desire to obtain relief from his suffering.

Thus, we see that the rich man prayed in the wrong place. He should have prayed and trusted God while on earth—not in hades. God would not answer the prayers of the rich man because he had sealed his own judgment. Death ends all opportunities for the unbeliever to accept Christ. That is why it is so important for us to make the most of our opportunities today. "Now is the accepted time; behold, now is the day of salvation" (II Cor. 6:2).

He Prayed to the Wrong Person

Besides praying in the wrong place, the rich man *prayed to the wrong person*. As a result, his prayers were not answered. Rather than praying to Jehovah, he prayed to Abraham. We read: "And he cried and said, Father Abraham, have mercy on me" (Luke 16:24).

In this passage it is important to note the significance of the phrase "Abraham's bosom" (see v. 22). In the Old Testament, the phrase "Abraham's bosom" was used by the Jewish people to denote paradise, the place where the faithful went after death. As the father of the Hebrew nation and a great man of faith, it seemed natural for Abraham to be waiting for the faithful Children of Israel after they died. The Jewish people took great pride in the fact that they were descendants of Abraham. In addition, it was the custom of the day for the most honored and respected guests at a feast to sit close to the host. The choicest position was that of leaning back on the host's bosom. Thus, in this passage, the Lord Jesus painted a beautiful picture. At his death, Lazarus (the poor, downtrodden beggar) was carried by the angels to the most honored place—Abraham's bosom. But the rich man, who

71

would have had an expensive funeral attended by many mourners, ended up in the most dishonored place—hades.

It would seem logical for the rich man to think that Abraham could do something for him. After all, he was a man of great faith, he was the friend of God, and he was a great intercessor. In fact, the Jews prided themselves on the fact that they were direct descendants of Abraham (see Matt. 3:9). But Abraham couldn't save the rich man; he was praying to the wrong person. In the same way, some people today believe that they can pray to people on the other side. However, I don't know of any verse of Scripture that instructs us to invoke the help of another person who has died and passed to the other side, whether in paradise or in hades. The only Person who can answer prayer is God. To pray to anyone else, dead or alive, is futile. Thus, the rich man prayed to the wrong person.

He Prayed for the Wrong Benefits

We see a third reason why the rich man's prayer wasn't answered. He not only prayed in the wrong place to the wrong person, he also *prayed for the wrong benefits*. What did he ask for? He wanted water. "Send Lazarus, that he may dip the tip of his finger in water, and cool my tongue; for I am tormented in this flame" (Luke 16:24).

This is a very interesting request when you remember that the rich man despised Lazarus. Previously he wouldn't have allowed Lazarus to touch him. But everything had changed. He would have given anything for a touch from Lazarus now. The same thing is true today. Those who don't know Christ as Saviour may want to have nothing to do with you. They may despise and reject you, especially if you try to witness to them. But one day they are going to wish they could see you. One day they are going to ache for some of the love and concern you tried to show them.

Even though the rich man asked for Lazarus to come, he really wanted something to alleviate his own pain. He was still selfish. But the irony of it all is that the water wouldn't have relieved his suffering anyway. The pain that people will endure in hell won't be alleviated by a little water.

We see God's law of compensation at work here. No, the rich man wasn't suffering because he had been happy during his life. He was suffering because he'd rejected God while he was alive. On the other hand, Lazarus—who had known pain and suffering during his lifetime—was now rejoicing in all the good things that were his. God does not promise His children comfort and ease during this life. But He does promise that one day they will be in His house (see John 14:1-3). There they will know eternal joy and will receive all of the blessings that He has prepared for them.

If the water had been given, it wouldn't have helped. But another reason his request was denied was because a great gulf was fixed between the rich man and Lazarus. Luke 16:26 tells us that once you wake up in the place of judgment there is no escape; also, no one can come from the place of joy and glory to do anything for you. So you must settle the matter of where you will spend eternity while you have the opportunity to do so. After you die, it's too late.

The rich man not only wanted water, but he also wanted a witness. When he finally realized that his condition was hopeless, he began to think of others. Perhaps this was the first time in his life that he had been concerned about helping someone else. He began to think of his five brothers and where they would spend eternity. He didn't want them to come to this place of torment. This man knew the reality of hades and hell. He was unlike many non-Christians today who think hell is a joke. If you tell them they're bound for hell, they respond, "That's OK. I'll have lots of company there." They have no idea of the terror and torment that awaits them if they choose to go there. They won't want lots of company then. They will beg and plead with God to do something so that their friends and loved ones won't join them. But no one has to experience the horror of hell if they trust the Lord Jesus to save them.

The rich man was asking for a miracle, but as with the water, it wouldn't have helped anyway. He said, in effect, "If someone came back from the dead, my brothers would repent and believe" (v. 30). No, they wouldn't. We have the example of Lazarus (Mary and Martha's brother), whom Jesus raised from the dead (see John 11:1-44). Those whose hearts were

74

hardened were not impressed when Lazarus came back from the dead. In fact, they plotted to kill him! (see 12:10). People are not saved because of miracles. They are saved when they become convicted by the Word of God.

Abraham told the rich man, "Your brothers have the witness of the Word of God—the Law and the Prophets. If they won't listen to that, nothing will change them" (see Luke 16:31). I like the word "persuaded" in verse 31: "Neither will they be persuaded, though one rose from the dead." God does not force people to trust Him. He gently persuades them. He wants us to know the truth about hell—that it is a place of suffering and torment—but He also wants us to see His heart of love. In order to keep us from going to hell, He sent His only Son to die for us. His Son took the suffering and punishment that should have been ours. He gently persuades us to trust Him and to yield our will to His.

The Lord could not answer the prayer of the rich man because he prayed in the wrong place, he prayed to the wrong person, and he prayed for the wrong benefits. Your prayers will go unheeded if you wait until you die to pray. The place to pray is on earth, and the time to pray is now. Likewise, you must make sure that your prayers are directed to the only One who can hear and answer them and that you are honestly seeking the Lord's will in your requests. You need to make the most of your opportunities today, including the opportunity to trust Christ as Saviour (if you are unsaved) or to serve Him (if you are a believer). No one knows how

75

long their life will be. Tomorrow could be eternally too late. Don't wait to call upon the name of the Lord. "For whosoever shall call upon the name of the Lord shall be saved" (Rom. 10:13).

Chapter 7

A Covetous Prayer

(Luke 12:13-21)

Someone has defined a bore as a person who is talking when you want to talk. This statement has a lot of truth to it. It is true that nobody likes to be interrupted. When I used to do street preaching, I often felt frustrated when someone would interrupt me to raise a question or to deny what I was preaching.

Even the Lord Jesus was not immune from interruptions during His messages. The Gospels record a number of such incidents. One example of this is found in Luke 12. Christ was preaching a sermon about the importance of trusting Him in the midst of adversity and of confessing Him before men (see vv. 1-12) when he was interrupted by a man who wanted Him to settle a dispute. We read: "And one of the company said unto him, Master, speak to my brother, that he divide the inheritance with me. And he said unto him, Man, who made me a judge or a divider over you [the two of you]?

"And he said unto them, Take heed, and beware of covetousness: for a man's life consisteth not in the abundance of the things which he possesseth.

And he spake a parable unto them, saying, The ground of a certain rich man brought forth plentifully: and he thought within himself, saying, What shall I do, because I have no room where to bestow my fruits [crops]? And he said, This will I do: I will pull down my barns, and build greater; and there will I bestow all my fruits and my goods. And I will say to my soul, Soul, thou hast much goods laid up for many years; take thine ease, eat, drink, and be merry. But God said unto him, Thou fool, this night thy soul shall be required of thee: then whose shall those things be, which thou hast provided? So is he that layeth up treasure for himself, and is not rich toward God" (vv. 13-21).

In the Jewish community of Christ's day, there was no distinction between church and state. The religious leaders were also the lawyers, judges and law enforcement officers. Thus, when the people had a family or neighborhood dispute, they would go to the local rabbi, and he was authorized to pass judgment. In the eyes of the Jews, Jesus was considered to be the great rabbi, or teacher (see John 1:38,49; 3:2; 20:16). However, when a man came to Jesus as He was preaching, He refused to hear his case. Why did He refuse to get involved in this family matter? Because the heart of the problem was the problem in the man's heart.

What if the Lord had listened to their case and had made a just and perfect decision, as only He could make? He still would not have solved the problem. Why? Because someone's heart would still have been wrong. Apparently, the other brother was selfish and greedy in not wanting to share the inheritance. However, the brother who made the request was just as selfish and grasping. The only difference was that he had nothing to grasp. Both men's hearts were wrong. When you make a judgment based on the outer circumstances without changing the inner attitudes, you only make the problem worse. The Lord realized this. Rather than addressing the issue of who should receive the inheritance, He instead went straight to the source of the dispute—their selfishness and greed.

We are living in an era when greed is rampant. Society tells us, "Look out for number one. Get what you deserve." Thus, our courts are filled with people who are suing others for exorbitant sums of money. Many of these cases are not motivated by justice or real need but by greed and selfishness. Jesus faced the same attitudes in His day. In Luke 12, and many other passages, He warned us about covetousness. In fact, His warning is so strong here that He used the word "beware" to emphasize the seriousness of this attitude (see v. 15). He told us that our lives should be directed toward service to God and others and not toward the accumulation of wealth, for it is only temporary.

Once again we find a person making a request of the Lord, and Jesus refusing to answer his prayer. In this passage, we discover that this man had a number of wrong attitudes in coming to Jesus. They were the cause of Christ's refusal to grant his request. Likewise, the source of many of our unanswered prayers are the improper motives behind our prayers. In order to understand what our attitude should be when we pray, let's compare this man's request with the Lord's Prayer, the model prayer Christ has given us (see Matt. 6:9-13).

Selfishness

When we compare the Lord's Prayer with the prayer of this man, we see, first of all, that the man was praying out of *selfishness* and not out of love for his brother or for the Father. The Lord's Prayer begins with the words, "Our Father which art in heaven" (Matt. 6:9). Notice that it is not *my* Father but *our* Father. The very first word in this prayer shows us that we belong to each other. Thus, when we pray, the needs of others should be uppermost in our minds.

However, this man's prayer was selfish from the beginning. He told Jesus, "Master, speak to my brother that he divide the inheritance with me" (Luke 12:13). He had the wrong attitude and motive behind his request. Instead of saying, "Lord, I am a part of the family, and my heart is broken at what is going on. Please help me to do what is right. Help me to love my brother," he demanded that the Lord Jesus force his brother to give him what he wanted. He had no real concern for the needs of his brother.

Jesus looked past the man's prayer to the heart of the problem—the problem in his heart. He told the man, "Who made me a judge or a divider over you?" (v. 14). This man's selfishness had blinded him not only to the needs of his brother but also to the character of Jesus. The Lord is our Father, not our judge. Christ came to earth to save people, not to condemn them (see John 3:16,17). He desires to deal with each of us, not as a criminal but as a child, in love and grace.

Because of this man's selfishness and misconceptions about the purpose of prayer and the character of Christ, the Lord refused to answer his prayer. Instead, He taught him an important lesson concerning what his attitude should be in prayer. He told the man, in effect, "You cannot pray 'our Father' when you are at odds with your brother."

Failure to Glorify God

A second reason why this man's prayer remained unanswered was because of his *failure to glorify God*. Bringing honor and glory to God is one of the primary purposes of prayer. Immediately following the opening salutation in the Lord's Prayer, we read: "Hallowed be thy name" (Matt. 6:9). When we pray, not only should we open our prayers with praise and adoration of God but also *every request we make should be the kind that will please and honor the Lord*.

In Luke 12 it would appear that this man belonged to the Jewish community. He knew Jehovah God and understood the Law. By making such a request of Christ, he was disgracing the name of God. In addition, he would have been setting a bad example for the other people. Perhaps there were some Gentiles in the crowd, listening to Jesus. This man not only interrupted Christ's message, possibly keeping some people from accepting Him, but his selfish demand also cast a bad light on "God's chosen race" and ultimately on the Lord Himself.

As Christ's representatives on earth, Christians must guard against doing anything that would cause others to reject the Lord. However, like this man, many believers today are dragging their disputes with family members and fellow believers into public. Does this glorify God's name? I don't think it does.

Regarding this issue, Paul admonished us, "Dare any of you, having a matter against another, go to law before the unjust, and not before the saints? Do ye not know that the saints shall judge the world? and if the world shall be judged by you, are ye unworthy to judge the smallest matters? . . . I speak to your shame. . . . But brother goeth to law with brother, and that before the unbelievers. Now therefore there is utterly a fault among you, because ye go to law one with another. Why do ye not rather take wrong? why do ye not rather suffer yourselves to be defrauded? Nay, ye do wrong, and defraud, and that your brethren" (I Cor. 6:1,2,5-8).

What is Paul saying to us in this passage? By dragging each other into court and suing our family and friends, we lose our testimony to unbelievers. The world sees no difference in us. We are just as selfish and greedy as other people. Not only have we ruined our chances of leading them to the Lord, but we have also publicly disgraced God's holy name. Thus, it is better to suffer injustice and loss than to air our grievances in public.

Abraham also realized the seriousness of this matter. When Lot was having a dispute with him over the division of the land, Abraham told him, "Let there be no strife, I pray thee, between me and thee, and between my herdmen and thy herdmen; for we be brethren" (Gen. 13:8).

Psalm 133:1 tells us, "Behold, how good and how pleasant it is for brethren to dwell together in unity!" We bring glory to God when we live in love and unity with our family and fellow believers. Likewise, when we are at odds with others, we cannot hallow God's name; thus, our prayers will not be answered.

Covetousness

In addition to his failure to glorify God and his selfish attitude, this man was also guilty of *covetousness*, a desire to have more. When we pray with this kind of spirit, the Lord will not answer our prayers.

What kind of attitude should we have in prayer? We should desire the Lord's will to be done and His kingdom to be advanced. We read in Matthew 6:10: "Thy kingdom come. Thy will be done in earth, as it is in heaven." It is evident that the man in Luke 12 was not interested in God's kingdom or in His will. He told the Lord, in effect, "I want *my* inheritance to come. I want *my* will to be done."

Because this man was so concerned with obtaining material wealth, he completely ignored Christ's sermon. If he had really heard the Lord's message, he never would have come to Him with such a request. This man, and many others, are illustra-

83

tions of Christ's parable of the sower (see Luke 8:5-15). Like seed that falls among the thorns, some people hear the Word but are so choked with the cares, riches and pleasures of this life that they bring no fruit to perfection (see v. 14). Many people sit in our churches on Sundays and don't really receive the seed of the Word of God. Why? Because their hearts are so crowded with the weeds of covetousness and of their desire for material possessions that they have no room for the Lord or His will.

Yes, we are instructed to pray for our needs. Immediately following the words "Thy will be done" in the Lord's Prayer, we read: "Give us this day our daily bread" (Matt. 6:11). But while it is not wrong to pray for our needs, our primary concern should be that of seeking the Lord's will in our lives. When we are praying in this manner, then He will meet our needs as well. In Matthew 6:33 Jesus instructed us, "But seek ye first the kingdom of God, and his righteousness; and all these things shall be added unto you."

However, while the Lord promises to give us what we need, He does not always give us what we want. When we begin to want more than we need, then we are in danger of committing the sin of covetousness. The word "covetousness" means "a desire for more." When the man came to Jesus, demanding that the Lord force his brother to divide the inheritance, it was not because he really needed it—he simply wanted more.

Jesus warned the man, and the rest of the crowd,

84

of the danger of covetousness (see Luke 12:15). To illustrate His point, Christ told the parable of the rich man. This man had just harvested a bumper crop and had no room to store it. Rather than using it to help others, he was only concerned with himself. Notice the number of personal pronouns in this passage: "What shall I do, because I have no room where to bestow my fruits? . . . This will I do: I will pull down my barns, and build greater; and there will I bestow all my fruits and my goods. And I will say to my soul, Soul, thou hast much goods laid up for many years; take thine ease, eat, drink, and be merry" (vv. 17-19). The pronouns "I" and "my" are used a total of 11 times. The tragedy is that while the man thought he was merely making a living and insuring a comfortable future, he was actually ruining his life and condemning himself to an eternity of suffering. God told him, "Thou fool, this night thy soul shall be required of thee: then whose shall those things be, which thou hast provided?" (v. 20).

Christ ended this parable with a severe warning: *Those who store up treasures for themselves on earth, rather than serving God, will suffer the same fate as the rich man* (see v. 21). Covetousness says to you, "Don't be satisfied with what you have. Grab everything you can get in life—even if you have to take it from your brother." This attitude is rampant in our society. It is dangerous because we can fall into this trap without realizing it. We begin to look at what others have, and the seed of desire is planted in our hearts. Then we begin to buy some of the "necessities" for a happy, comfortable life. Soon we are working longer hours and cheating God out of the time and money He deserves, believing that we are merely "providing for our family."

While covetousness tells us to possess everything we can in life, Christ said to us, "Take no thought for your life, what ye shall eat; neither what ye shall put on" (v. 22). He added that worrying about these things will not help the situation. Instead, we need to trust God. When doing God's will and working in His kingdom are what matter most to us, then He will see that we have what we need as well (see vv. 23-34).

Lack of Forgiveness

A fourth reason why Jesus did not answer this man's prayer is because he demonstrated a *lack of forgiveness*. Apparently their father had died, and now the two brothers were fighting over their inheritance. Families are often divided over an inheritance. Siblings often quarrel over what they feel is rightfully theirs. A will can bring out the worst in people, and divisions can result that take years to heal. Apparently the man who came to Jesus felt his brother was defrauding him in this matter of his inheritance, and he wouldn't forgive him. If this man had demonstrated a spirit of forgiveness, he would have come to Jesus privately and said, "Master, I have a great burden on my heart. My brother is defrauding me. I love him and don't want to cause a scandal. Would you pray for my brother and for me? Help me to love him and to help him so that we can glorify God."

The Lord's Prayer says, "Forgive us our debts, as we forgive our debtors" (Matt. 6:12). If the Lord forgave us as we forgive others, where would we be in our relationship with Him? Do you know why God has instructed us to forgive others? Because failing to do so hurts *us*. One of Satan's tricks is to cause us to believe that holding a grudge against someone hurts that person and atones for what he did to us. If you want to have an enemy, you'd better find a good one because enemies are very expensive. They will cause you all kinds of grief. They will rob you of sleep, and they will rob you of peace. This is one reason why God's Word tells us that it's better to allow ourselves to be defrauded than to take our brother to court and fight for what is ours (see I Cor. 6:7).

Of course, the best thing to do is not to have any enemies, to forgive others even though they may have hurt you deeply. But this man wouldn't forgive his brother. He was convinced his brother was at fault. It couldn't possibly be *his* fault. So often in our prayers we pray about those who have hurt us. We never say, "Father, have I hurt anyone? Should I stop praying and go to someone and ask him (or her) to forgive me?"

The Lord's Prayer continues by saying, "Lead us not into temptation, but deliver us from evil [the Evil One]" (Matt. 6:13). This man was playing right into the hands of the Devil by failing to forgive. In Ephesians 4:26,27 we read: "Be ye angry, and sin not: let not the sun go down upon your wrath: neither give place to the devil." This man was giving Satan a perfect opportunity to destroy his family and his own relationship with God. He was angry with his brother and was holding a grudge against him. He should have gone to his brother and said, "Brother, you've hurt me, and I am angry. But let's work this matter out. Let's talk to Jesus together and try to settle it."

Ephesians 4 goes on to say, "Grieve not the [Holy] Spirit of God. . . . Let all bitterness, and wrath, and anger, and clamour, and evil speaking, be put away from you, with all malice: and be ye kind one to another, tenderhearted, forgiving one another, even as God for Christ's sake hath forgiven you" (vv. 30-32). Here God tells us what to do to prevent the Devil from gaining an opportunity. We are to put away all bitterness, anger and malice. Malice is that cancer of the soul that eats away at us, spreading poison throughout our system and making us so hard to live with. Instead, we are to be kind to one another and to forgive each other. God has given us the example to follow. When we remember how many times and how much He has forgiven us, we dare not hold a grudge against a brother.

"Lead us not into temptation" (Matt. 6:13). The desire for material wealth is often a source of temptation. Paul wrote: "The love of money is the root of all [kinds of] evil" (I Tim. 6:10). Did you realize that covetousness causes a person to break all the other commandments? The last commandment is "Thou shalt not covet" (Ex. 20:17). If a person covets, he will start being an idolater (see vv. 3-5). In fact, Colossians 3:5 tells us that covetousness is idolatry.

Why? Because we are putting *things* in the place of God. If a person is covetous, he will lie to obtain what he wants. He will steal (see Ex. 20:15). He will even commit adultery (see v. 14). He will bear false witness (see v. 16). He will dishonor his own family to obtain his desires (see v. 12). So the desire to possess more and more will cause us to break other commandments and will lead us deeper into sin.

Rather than allowing ourselves to be led into temptation, we are to ask God to "deliver us from evil: For thine is the kingdom" (Matt. 6:13). Since all things are under God's control, we can trust Him. He can work the problem out. He can give us far more than anyone can take from us. "Thine is . . . the power" (v. 13). Not only is everything under God's sovereign control, but He also possesses the power necessary to do what He promises. He has the power to take care of our needs so that we will never be in want. We should let that power work in our lives. "Thine is . . . the glory" (v. 13). Here is often where the real problem lies when we come to God in prayer. Who is going to be glorified? If God will be glorified, we can pray with confidence. But if I only want my own way so that I can brag about what I received, that's quite another matter. We can be sure God will not answer our prayer.

"Thine is the kingdom, and the power, and the glory, for ever" (v. 13). A hundred years from now what will this situation look like in the light of eternity? Will you regret the wrong attitudes you displayed? Will you regret making such an issue of such a small matter? Some things that appear so important and so crucial to us seem petty in the light of eternity. Examine the situations you are worried about and maybe even fighting about. In the light of eternity is this problem worth the time and energy you're giving it?

It is obvious that the man who brought his request to Jesus did not know much about the One he was coming to. His request falls far short of the guidelines given to us in the Lord's Prayer. The Lord refused to grant his request for several reasons. First, the man was selfish. He didn't realize that the problem was in his own heart. He was looking only at his brother and at how much he was being cheated. Second, this man failed to glorify God. It didn't matter to him that he was dragging a family dispute before the public. He was only thinking of his wants and his comfort. This man was also covetous. What he had didn't matter; he wanted more. He would not allow his brother to cheat him out of so much as a penny. Finally, this man was giving the Devil a tremendous opportunity for victory because of his lack of forgiveness of his brother. His love of money had led him into temptation and into all kinds of evil. We need to be careful if money or material possessions become too important to us. Our desires will lead us to commit other sins and will also harm our relationship with the Lord so that He cannot answer our prayers.

Mark Twain once said, "Civilization is a limitless multiplication of unnecessary necessities." I think that is true. We can become so wrapped up in things that we begin to think material possessions are our life. They are not. Our Lord warned, "Take heed, and beware of covetousness: for a man's life consisteth not in the abundance of the things which he possesseth" (Luke 12:15).

Chapter 8

The High Cost of Prayer
(Matthew 20:20-28)

Any Christian who takes prayer seriously eventually faces the disappointment of unanswered prayer. When this happens, people respond differently. Some argue with God. Others become angry with Him, revolting against His will and leaving the church. Still others react with quiet bitterness, allowing their lives to be poisoned with disappointment and dejection. Some continue to pray bravely, hoping that somehow something will happen. Because we will all face the trauma of unanswered prayer at some point in our lives, we must learn to deal realistically with this matter.

When we are grappling with the problem of unanswered prayer, we need to remember, first of all, that we are not alone. As we have seen, some of God's greatest servants experienced unanswered prayer at times. In each case, we saw specific reasons for the Lord's refusal to answer. Generally, the heart of the problem was the problem in their heart, whether it was selfishness, covetousness, lack of forgiveness or some other sin. When we receive a no from God, it is usually because we have some problem in our life that is hindering our prayers. However, at times the Lord does choose not to answer our prayers because He has some greater purpose in mind, as in the case of Elijah and the healed demoniac. And, as we shall see in this chapter, frequently our prayers are not answered because we have the wrong attitude toward prayer.

In Matthew 20 we find the prayer of James, John and their mother, Salome, and Christ's response to their request. We read: "Then came to him the mother of Zebedee's children with her sons, worshipping him, and desiring a certain thing of him. And he said unto her, What wilt thou? She saith unto him, Grant that these my two sons may sit, the one on thy right hand, and the other on the left, in thy kingdom.

"But Jesus answered and said, Ye know not what ye ask. Are ye able to drink of the cup that I shall drink of, and to be baptized with the baptism that I am baptized with? They say unto him, We are able. And he saith unto them, Ye shall drink indeed of my cup, and be baptized with the baptism that I am baptized with: but to sit on my right hand, and on my left, is not mine to give, but it shall be given to them for whom it is prepared of my Father.

"And when the ten heard it, they were moved with indignation against the two brethren. But Jesus called them unto him, and said, Ye know that the princes of the Gentiles exercise dominion [lord it] over them, and they that are great exercise authority upon them. But it shall not be so among

93

you: but whosoever will be great among you, let him be your minister; and whosoever will be chief among you, let him be your servant: even as the Son of man came not to be ministered unto, but to minister, and to give his life a ransom for many" (vv. 20-28).

James and John were faithful and devoted disciples of Jesus. However, we see in this passage that they had a problem with pride. Their prayer was motivated, in part, by their pride. In fact, they were so sure that Christ would give them their request that they asked for it publicly. However, the Lord did not answer their request because He realized that they had misconceptions about the purpose of His ministry and the purpose of prayer. He told them, "You don't know what you are asking. Are you able to endure what I will suffer?" (see v. 22). If James and John had really understood the purpose of Christ's kingdom and His prophecies about the events to come (see vv. 17-19), they never would have made this request. While they did not receive the privilege of sitting on His right and left, they did drink of the same cup as Jesus. James was the first of the 12 apostles to be martyred. King Herod had him beheaded (see Acts 12:1,2). John was severely persecuted, imprisoned a number of times and finally banished to the island of Patmos, where he died (see Rev. 1:9).

Prayer Involves Relationships—Not Rules

From this experience Jesus taught the disciples (and us) three important, and surprising, lessons

94

about the purpose of prayer and what our attitude should be in prayer. First, we learn that *prayer involves relationships—not rules.*

We live in a world that is very formula oriented. This mentality is due, in large part, to science. Our society is very mechanized and logical. We have learned that if we push A, B and C, we will get D. Scientists teach us that everything has a logical explanation, which is found by using reason and by following the rules of science.

Christians are often guilty of this type of thinking when it comes to their spiritual lives as well. They become wrapped up in formulas—five steps for being filled with the Holy Spirit, eight steps for solving problems—believing that by following these rules, they will be successful in their walk with the Lord. We have even devised formulas for how to pray. We follow a particular order—adoration of God, confession of sin, thanksgiving and supplication for others and for ourselves—and obey certain "rules" of prayer, such as being specific and praying in faith. People have written or phoned me and said, "Brother Wiersbe, we have gone through all these steps, and we are still in the same mess. What's wrong?" To them, my answer is simply this: *The Christian life is not rules and regulations—it's relationships.* This is especially true of prayer.

While these rules and formulas for prayer are good to follow, they do not automatically guarantee that our prayers will be answered. We notice in Matthew 20 that Salome and her two sons obeyed all the rules of prayer. First, we see that they had the right attitude. They began by worshiping the Lord (see v. 20). Second, they were specific in their request. The problem with so many prayers today is that they are too general. We pray, "Lord, bless our pastor and the missionaries around the world. Grant that we may have peace everywhere." Then we wonder why we never see our prayers being answered! God's Word instructs us to be specific when we pray. In the Lord's Prayer, our model for prayer, we find specific requests for provision of our daily needs, for help in temptation and for forgiveness, among others (see 6:9-13).

Not only did they have the right attitude in prayer and make a specific request, but they also claimed a promise. This, too, is an important aspect of prayer. What promise were Salome and her sons claiming? Shortly before this incident, Jesus had told the Twelve, "Verily I say unto you, That ye which have followed me, in the regeneration when the Son of man shall sit in the throne of his glory, ye also shall sit upon twelve thrones, judging the twelve tribes of Israel" (19:28). Salome remembered this promise and was claiming it for her sons. She said, in effect, "I remember what You said, Lord. Since You have promised that the disciples will sit on thrones in Your kingdom, may my sons have the places of honor on Your right and left?"

Furthermore, these three followers of Jesus had faith. How do we know they had faith? Because of what Jesus had just predicted (see 20:17-19). The Lord had just told His disciples about His coming betrayal, crucifixion and resurrection on the third day. Even though they didn't understand the purpose of His death or His kingdom, they believed that Christ would keep His promise to make them rulers, in spite of His death on the cross. It took great faith to believe that Jesus could come back to life and establish His kingdom as He had promised.

In addition, Salome, James and John agreed about their request. Earlier, the Lord had also told them, "If two of you shall agree on earth as touching any thing that they shall ask, it shall be done for them of my Father which is in heaven" (18:19). Since they were in agreement about what they wanted, it only seemed natural to them that Christ would answer their prayer.

Thus, we see that Salome and her sons had met all the "conditions" for answered prayer. They had the right attitude of worship. Their request was specific. They claimed Christ's promise and had faith that He would perform it. And they were agreed in their request. Yet Jesus did not answer their prayer. Why? Because their relationships were wrong. We can follow every "rule" of prayer, but if our relationship with the Lord and with others is not what it should be, then our prayers will not be answered.

How were their relationships wrong? We see, first of all, that James, John and Salome each had *a wrong relationship to himself*. Every one of them wanted to have a place of importance. Salome wanted the recognition that would come if her sons had honored positions in Christ's kingdom. And

James and John wanted to be more powerful and favored than the other disciples.

In addition, this mother and her sons had *a wrong relationship to each other*. Salome was indulging her sons. She wasn't concerned about building their character or making them better people; she merely wanted to please them. Likewise, James and John may have been using their mother to get what they wanted. They probably didn't have the nerve to make such a request of Jesus for themselves, so they had their mother do it for them. But the Lord told them that they could not earn the honored places through their own preparation or promotion. The thrones were for those who had been prepared by the Father (see 20:23).

Salome and her sons also had *a wrong relationship to the disciples*. They forgot that other people were involved in their prayer. They didn't stop to think about the consequences of their request and what it would do to their relationship with the other disciples. We see that it did, in fact, create some strife among the Twelve (see v. 24).

Finally, we see that they had *a wrong relationship with the Lord*. From their request it is evident that they were ignorant of the will of God and of the price that is paid for answered prayer. If they had really known Jesus, they would have realized that He loves everyone equally. He does not play favorites. And He will not answer a prayer that will hurt someone else in the process.

Thus, the key word in prayer is "submit." We build relationships by submitting to others. When we have a true relationship with a person, we know that person inside and out. We have a close bond with him that allows us to know what he is thinking and feeling. Because we love him, we want to do what will please him. This is the kind of relationship we are to have with the Lord. The closer we are to Him, the better we will know what He wants us to do. We can then pray according to the Lord's will, resulting in answered prayer.

Prayer Involves Taking—Not Giving—Orders

When you are facing unanswered prayer, you need to remember first that prayer involves relationships—not rules. If your relationship with the Lord and with others is not what it should be, then your prayers will be hindered. The second important lesson we need to learn is that *prayer involves taking orders—not giving them.* Often people have the mistaken idea that God is a cosmic bellhop or an errand boy. Prayer becomes a bargaining table where we tell the Lord, "If You keep Your end of the bargain, I'll keep mine." However, prayer is not a commercial relationship with our Father in heaven. We do not bargain for what we want.

Salome and her two sons had a false view of the purpose of prayer. Rather than telling God what He must do for you, prayer involves first coming to Him and saying, "I am available, Lord. 'Hallowed be thy name. Thy kingdom come. Thy will be done in earth, as it is in heaven,' and start with me."

If James, John and Salome had come to Christ and said, "Lord Jesus, we worship You, and we

99

want to be Your servants. What do You want us to do?" the situation would have changed entirely. Are you a servant in prayer? Prayer does not give us the right to climb up on a throne and tell other people what to do. Instead, prayer is making ourselves available to God that He might work in us and through us. "Now unto him that is able to do exceeding abundantly above all that we ask or think, according to the power that worketh in us" (Eph. 3:20). When we willingly follow the orders of Christ rather than issuing orders, His power will work in our lives far beyond what we could ever ask, or even imagine.

Prayer Involves Giving—Not Getting

The third vital lesson we must learn is that *prayer involves giving—not just getting.* Of course, we do receive much through prayer, and part of the purpose of prayer is to ask God for what we need: "Give us this day our daily bread" (Matt. 6:11). However, if we are only receiving, without giving in return, then our prayers—and God's answers—often become cheap.

In the wilderness, the Israelites cried out to God, "We are tired of manna. Give us some meat to eat" (see Num. 11:4-6,16-20,31-33). God granted their request, sending quail from heaven. However, He also sent leanness to their souls (see Ps. 106:14,15). It would have been better for their prayer not to have been answered. While they had their physical desires fulfilled, their spiritual lives suffered.

Have you come to the point where you are thankful for unanswered prayer? Look at some of the requests on your prayer list. Do you really want what you are asking for? What if God were to give you everything you requested? Would it be a cheap answer to a cheap prayer?

We must realize that prayer is costly—both for God and for us. When James and John requested to have the places of honor in Christ's kingdom, Jesus looked at them and said, in effect, "Do you know what it is going to cost Me to prepare a throne for you? I will have to shed My blood on a cross so that you can have the privilege of serving Me and one day reigning with Me in Glory." The Lord had to pay a tremendous price for us to live and reign with Him. Likewise, it costs God something to answer our prayers. In answering our prayers, God has to work in us—and for us—in order that He might be able to work through us to accomplish His will.

Many times God refuses to answer our shallow, selfish prayers, because to do so would deprive us of deeper, more meaningful blessings later. In addition, He may not answer our prayers because we are not ready for the answer. Jesus could have given James and John the thrones of honor, but He knew they were not ready for them yet. They needed to be tempered and purified by the fire of adversity first.

Being successful when you are not ready for success leads to tragedy. I've seen this happen often in the ministry. A person goes into the ministry unprepared for the amount of work, for the exposure and for the praise and applause he will receive

101

and ends up ruining himself and his ministry. Why? Because he succeeded before he was ready.

The beauty of prayer is that God prepares us for what He is preparing for us. When we have developed that special relationship with the Lord and are constantly seeking His will in prayer, He will not answer our prayers until He has fully prepared us to receive and use the answer.

Many times this preparation involves using us to answer our prayers. For example, if we ask God to save a friend or loved one, we need to be prepared to be the one He uses to bring that person to Himself. Often the key to receiving answers to our prayers lies in our willingness to give of ourselves in order to make the answer possible. When Moses was burdened for the Israelites and prayed for their release, the Lord called him to deliver them (see Ex. 3:7-10). Likewise, when Nehemiah prayed for the great needs in Jerusalem, God sent him to the city to help the people (see Neh. 1:5-11; 2:11).

When James and John requested the privilege of sitting next to Jesus on the throne, little did they know what it would cost them. Jesus told them that the road to greatness is paved with servanthood. He stated, "Whosoever will be great among you, let him be your minister; and whosoever will be chief among you, let him be your servant" (Matt. 20:26,27). In order to be first, we must first be last. In order to be served, we must first serve. And the place to begin our service is at the throne of grace, where we bow and say, "Not my will but Thy will be done."

If our prayer life has made us selfish and demanding, then something is wrong with our prayer life. I think Salome and her sons learned this lesson. Shortly after this incident, we find Salome and John standing at the foot of the cross (see Mark 15:40; John 19:25,26). As they stood there looking up at Jesus, I imagine they remembered their recent request for prestige and power and realized just how wrong it was.

Have you ever taken your prayer request to the cross and measured it by Calvary? It can be a very humbling experience. What you thought was so important often seems insignificant and petty compared to what Christ has already given you.

In the request of Salome and her sons, we learn an important truth about prayer: *Answered prayer is not cheap for God or for us. If we want to receive answers to our prayers, we must be willing to pay the cost.* First, we must be willing to spend the time and energy necessary to build proper relationships with God and with others, for prayer is a relationship—not a list of rules and formulas. Second, we must be willing to take orders rather than give them. Our prayer time should not be a bargaining session where we make demands of God. Instead, we should pray, asking the Lord to accomplish His will in us, and then wait for Him to tell us what to do. Third, we must be willing to be the instrument God uses to fulfill our request, for prayer involves giving as well as receiving. When we have learned these important lessons, we will then begin to experience the joy of answered prayer.

Chapter 9

Prayer and Suffering

(II Corinthians 12:1-10)

In many of the examples of unanswered prayer we have examined, we can easily see why the Lord did not answer. The man who came to Jesus with a complaint about his brother prayed a covetous prayer. James, John and Salome prayed a selfish prayer. But it's not so easy to understand why the Lord would deny the request of someone like the Apostle Paul when he prayed for healing. We read about it in II Corinthians 12: "It is not expedient for me doubtless to glory. I will come to visions and revelations of the Lord. I knew a man in Christ above fourteen years ago, (whether in the body, I cannot tell; or whether out of the body, I cannot tell: God knoweth;) such an one caught up to the third heaven. And I knew such a man, (whether in the body, or out of the body, I cannot tell: God knoweth;) how that he was caught up into paradise, and heard unspeakable words, which it is not lawful for a man to utter. Of such an one will I glory: yet of myself I will not glory, but in mine infirmities. For though I would desire to glory, I shall not be a fool;

for I will say the truth: but now I forbear, lest any man should think of me above that which he seeth me to be, or that he heareth of me.

"And lest I should be exalted above measure through the abundance of the revelations, there was given to me a thorn in the flesh, the messenger of Satan to buffet me, lest I should be exalted above measure. For this thing I besought the Lord thrice, that it might depart from me. And he said unto me, My grace is sufficient for thee: for my strength is made perfect in weakness. Most gladly therefore will I rather glory in my infirmities, that the power of Christ may rest upon me. Therefore I take pleasure in infirmities, in reproaches, in necessities, in persecutions, in distresses for Christ's sake: for when I am weak, then am I strong" (vv. 1-10).

The Corinthians were very proud and back-slidden believers. They had even begun to attack Paul and his apostolic authority. So he felt compelled to share with them—even to boast a little about—some evidences of his call to apostleship. He told them about his background and about the hardships he had endured in his defense of the Gospel. Then he began to share with them how he had even been permitted to behold the glory of the heavenly realm. This was such an extraordinary honor that the Lord had given Paul a physical affliction to keep him from becoming too proud.

As Paul shared these things with the Corinthians, he used a bit of holy irony. The Corinthians had been glorying in all of their blessings, so Paul said, "I could glory about having gone to heaven. For 14

105

years I've kept quiet about it. I could glory in that special revelation, but instead I'm going to glory in my infirmities."

Paul had prayed three times that his physical affliction would be removed, but his prayer was not answered. You might think that if anyone would receive answers to his prayers, it would be the Apostle Paul, but his prayer was not answered. It is interesting to note that Paul prayed three times, just as our Lord Jesus did in Gethsemane (see Matt. 26:36-46). Just as the Father did not spare the Son from the suffering He had to endure, God did not remove Paul's affliction; instead, He gave them both the grace necessary to bear the suffering for His glory. And Paul began to learn that God had allowed his affliction for a specific purpose. Let's look more closely at Paul's experience of unanswered prayer and see what valuable lessons we can learn from it.

Afflictions Have a Divine Purpose

The first lesson we can learn from Paul's experience is that *afflictions have a divine purpose.* Not all afflictions come from God however. Sometimes we bring physical ailments upon ourselves. We should not be surprised if we contract a disease by failing to practice godly moral standards. If we do not eat the right foods, we can develop deficiencies that lead to illnesses. Sometimes habits, such as smoking or drinking, are harmful or damaging to our bodies. Of course, we usually don't stop to evaluate our wrong actions until we face the consequences. Then we often cry out to God, "Oh, God, I will never do that again." However, if we recover from the affliction, we often go right back and do it again. How unfortunate it is when Christians bring trials upon themselves!

But sometimes God does allow afflictions to come into our lives through no fault of our own. In Paul's case God permitted Satan to do in a limited way to Paul what he had done to Job. We do not know for sure what Paul's affliction was. We do know it was a physical problem of some kind because he called it a "thorn in the flesh" (II Cor. 12:7). Satan was not disturbing him mentally or emotionally. He was afflicting him physically with a problem that was a constant irritation. Paul referred to it as "the messenger of Satan to buffet me" (v. 7).

When God allows the affliction, He has a divine purpose for doing so. Sometimes He wants to *correct* us, sometimes He wants to *perfect* us, and sometimes He wants to *protect* us. Hebrews 12 helps us to understand why God must correct us at times. When we sin, God must discipline us because He is a loving Father. Hebrews 12 refers to this as chastening: "Whom the Lord loveth he chasteneth" (v. 6). Every loving parent knows the value of discipline in the life of a child. If the child is to learn to distinguish right from wrong, he must be disciplined. While the punishment is never pleasant, it helps the child to remember what is acceptable behavior. Parents use discipline to break the selfish, rebellious will of the child. While loving parents use discipline to accomplish good purposes, God has a

107

higher goal in mind—that of perfecting us in holiness. "They [earthly parents] verily for a few days chastened us after their own pleasure; but he [God] for our profit, that we might be partakers of his holiness" (v. 10).

Sometimes God wants to perfect us. He permits afflictions to come, not because we've done something wrong but because He wants us to do something right. He allows us to go through the furnace of affliction to refine us. Just as heating an imperfect metal causes the impurities to surface so that they can be skimmed away, the trial causes the imperfections in our faith to be revealed to us. "Wherein ye greatly rejoice, though now for a season, if need be, ye are in heaviness through manifold temptations: that the trial of your faith, being much more precious than of gold that perisheth, though it be tried with fire, might be found unto praise and honour and glory at the appearing of Jesus Christ" (I Pet. 1:6,7).

Sometimes the afflictions are allowed in order to protect us. This was God's purpose in Paul's case. God allowed Paul to have the thorn in the flesh to keep him from becoming too proud about the fact that he had been to heaven and come back. Pride is a terrible sin. Pride is the sin that turned Lucifer (the most splendid archangel) into Satan (see Isa. 14:12-17). Success and spiritual blessing can sometimes be a great hazard. We begin to take the blessings for granted, and we become careless spiritually. We may forget what God has done for us and begin to boast of what we have accomplished. The Lord warned the Israelites of this very thing before they went in to possess the land: "When thou hast eaten and art full, then thou shalt bless the Lord thy God for the good land which he hath given thee. Beware that thou forget not the Lord thy God, in not keeping his commandments, and his judgments, and his statutes, which I command thee this day: lest when thou hast eaten and art full, and hast built goodly houses, and dwelt therein; and when thy herds and thy flocks multiply, and thy silver and thy gold is multiplied, and all that thou hast is multiplied; then thine heart be lifted up, and thou forget the Lord thy God" (Deut. 8:10-14). When the Lord sees that we are growing spiritually and are having success, He may permit affliction in our lives to keep us from becoming proud.

Afflictions have a divine purpose, whether it is to correct us, perfect us or protect us. When we are facing affliction and when we know we have not brought it upon ourselves, our first question should not be "How can I get out of this?" but rather "What can I get out of this? What is God trying to accomplish?" If we can understand God's design, it will be easier to accept the affliction and allow it to accomplish its intended purpose.

Blessings Are Balanced With Burdens

A second lesson we can learn from Paul's experience of unanswered prayer is that *blessings are balanced with burdens.* Our Father in heaven keeps everything in perfect balance. He knows how to balance the seasons. He knows how to balance

109

day and night. He knows how to balance blessings with burdens and visions with trials. That is what He did with Paul. He allowed Paul—whether in the body or out of the body we don't know—to go to heaven where he saw glorious sights and heard wonderful words.

If I were allowed to have such an experience, I imagine I'd call a press conference when I came back. Maybe I would write a book or produce a series of films or cassettes. Perhaps I would start a seminar on how to prepare for the glory of heaven! But Paul didn't do that. He didn't tell anyone about the honor that had been his. For 14 years he was afflicted as a result of that experience, and yet he did not tell people why he had that affliction.

I can just imagine what Paul's enemies must have said. He would be ministering to believers, and his enemies would be there. This legalistic crowd that opposed the message of God's grace would say, "Did you notice? Paul has an affliction. If he were a good Christian, if he had enough faith, he wouldn't have this problem. I wonder why he has that affliction?" They might have even confronted Paul about his "backslidden" condition. If they did, he could have answered, "I have this affliction because I am so close to the Lord. I've been to heaven and back. Have you ever done that?" But Paul kept his mouth shut. He hadn't told anyone until the Corinthians forced him to defend his apostleship.

When God has given a person great blessings, He often has to balance this with great burdens. God knows that if He continuously fills my hands with blessings, eventually I will fall on my face! So as He fills my hands with blessings, He also places burdens on my back. In this way He keeps me balanced and poised so that I don't fall over. The Lord knows how to keep the load exactly balanced. He never gives me a burden greater than I can bear.

We can even see this principle at work in the life of the Lord Jesus when He was on earth. You will remember that He was baptized by John the Baptist. As He came up out of the water, He saw the Holy Spirit descending on Him like a dove (Matt. 3:16) and He heard His Father say, "This is my beloved Son, in whom I am well pleased" (v. 17). What a glorious experience that must have been! But the very next verse says, "Then was Jesus led up of the spirit [Holy Spirit] into the wilderness to be tempted of the devil" (4:1). After fasting for 40 days, He was tempted three times by Satan. So the blessing of His baptism was balanced by the testing of Satan.

It's normal for us to want only blessings and victories in life. But you can't reach the mountain-top without passing through the valley. And the air is pretty thin up on the mountaintop; you couldn't live there forever. Likewise, no one has ever had a victory celebration without having fought and won the battle. If you are going to claim the spoils of victory, you must first become involved in the battle. And the thrill of victory is even sweeter once you've known the agony of defeat.

Of course, few people can emerge from a battle unscathed. In order to experience victory, we must

111

first endure the pain and discomfort of the battle. No one enjoys pain and defeat. We have all prayed at one time or another, "Lord, heal my body. Take away this pain." Paul prayed this way, and nothing is wrong with doing that. But if God doesn't answer that prayer, don't despair and think He doesn't care about you. Remember that afflictions have a divine purpose and that blessings are always balanced with burdens. God does not want any pampered children. Instead, He wants us to grow.

Spiritual Blessings Surpass Physical Blessings

A third lesson we can learn from Paul's unanswered prayer is that *spiritual blessings are more important than physical blessings.* Of course, this does not mean that God is not concerned about the physical. He purchased our body, as well as our soul and spirit, at the cross. When we are saved, the Holy Spirit comes in to seal our conversion and to make our body His temple (see I Cor. 6:19,20). Thus, the Holy Spirit dwells within our physical being.

For this reason, Christians are instructed by God to take care of their bodies—His temple. However, the Lord often seems to be more concerned about our bodies than we are. We frequently do not care for them as we should. While the Lord does desire to keep us physically safe and sound, He is far more concerned with our spiritual condition. Spiritual blessings are more important to Him than physical ones. We should have this same attitude. Our first concern should be our spiritual well-being, not our

112

physical comfort and happiness (see Rom. 8:5-13).

Of course, God can—and does—heal us. I believe that He can heal every affliction—except the last one. When the Lord has chosen to call us home, He will not answer our prayers for healing. God has the power to heal every disease; however, He is not obligated to do so. While we have inherited every blessing through the cross, this does not mean that we will experience all these blessings while on earth. For example, we know that we will receive a resurrection body because of Calvary, but we will not inherit this body until the Lord returns (see v. 23).

Many times the Lord chooses not to answer our prayers for healing or for some other physical blessing because to do so would deprive us of an even greater spiritual blessing. We can see this in the experience of the Apostle Paul. God did something far greater for him than healing his "thorn in the flesh." The Lord used it to build his character.

Recently I received a letter from a dear radio listener, who told me of how she had gone through severe suffering and trials. She said, "God has not healed me, but He's done something even greater. He has used this affliction to bless me spiritually."

Not only does the Lord use our physical afflictions to bless us spiritually, but when we are called to experience suffering, He also gives us the grace to accept and endure our weakness. When Paul prayed three times for relief from his affliction, the Lord told him, "My grace is sufficient for thee: for my strength is made perfect in weakness" (II Cor. 12:9). The Lord gave Paul enough grace to accept,

113

understand and even glory in his weakness. In fact, His grace was sufficient enough to turn Paul's weakness into strength. When the apostle realized that his affliction allowed Christ's power to work through him, he was able to take pleasure in his weakness for Jesus' sake rather than complain about it (see v. 9).

I think it is far more important for God to *convert* our pain than it is for Him to *heal* our pain. When God's grace enables the believer to rejoice in his suffering rather than complain about it, the unsaved world is greatly affected by this powerful testimony. Often the Lord is glorified more by allowing us to be afflicted than He would be if He chose to heal us.

Afflictions Are No Barrier to Service

As we have seen, afflictions have a divine purpose that is more important than physical blessings. While the Lord does bless us richly, He balances those blessings with burdens so we do not fall. But, as we struggle with the burdens, we must also remember that *afflictions are no barrier to service*.

The Apostle Paul suffered greatly with his "thorn in the flesh." When he did not receive healing, it would have been easy for him to quit the ministry, rationalizing that his illness was preventing him from serving God effectively. However, he did not do this. Once he learned that the Lord was not going to heal him, he did not continue asking to escape his problem or to simply endure it. Instead, he prayed that he might be able to invest his problem and use it for the glory of God.

114

We live in an "aspirin" age. Too many Christians use pain and suffering as an excuse for not serving the Lord. How often do church members miss Sunday services because of some small ache or pain? How often do we use a headache or some other discomfort as an excuse for skipping a board meeting or choir rehearsal? Rather than using suffering as a scapegoat, we should instead be seeking ways to employ it in God's service.

History is brimming with examples of those who have served God effectively in spite of—and because of—their afflictions. Jacob had a limp for most of his adult life—obtained in a wrestling match with the Lord (see Gen. 32:24-31). His many beatings, stonings and imprisonments left Paul weak and in poor health, yet he served the Lord tirelessly. David Brainerd, missionary to the Indians in the 1740s, was reported to have been so ill at times that you could tell where he had been riding by the blood he had spit up on the snow. Robert Murray McCheyne, the godly Presbyterian preacher, had severe heart problems, yet he ministered very effectively. Charles Spurgeon and G. Campbell Morgan both had afflictions as well. Amy Carmichael, whose books have been a blessing to many, spent most of her ministry in bed. The lives of these men and women, and many others like them, show us that afflictions are no barrier to service.

When God does not answer our prayers and heal as we think He should, we need to remember that "it is a greater thing to pray for pain's conversion than for its removal" (P. T. Forsyth). We should seek God's will and divine purpose in our afflictions. He may be using our burdens as a means of blessing us spiritually or of bringing glory to Himself. Whatever the reason, we should not allow our suffering to hinder our service. We should discover what the Lord wants us to do, and then strive to do it, remembering that His grace and power is sufficient for our weakness.

Back to the Bible is a nonprofit ministry dedicated to Bible teaching, evangelism and edification of Christians worldwide.

If we may assist you in knowing more about Christ and the Christian life, please write to us without obligation:

Back to the Bible
P.O. Box 82808
Lincoln, NE 68501